W9-AAT-421

CULTURES OF THE WORLD®

NETHERLANDS

Pat Seward & Sunandini Arora Lal

MARSHALL CAVENDISH BENCHMARK

PICTURE CREDITS

Cover: © Adina Tovy / Art Directors
Aeroview (Dick Sellenraad): 17, 31 • Bes Stock: 1, 5, 6, 30, 38, 48, 51, 55, 56, 78, 120, 130 • Eric Goosen: 32 • HBL: 3, 77, 85, 100, 110, 112, 128 • ImageHub: 58 • The Image Bank: 16, 26, 40, 44, 61, 62, 91 • International Photobank: 4, 20, 25, 29, 46, 82 • Life File Photo Library: 19, 28, 63, 69 • Marshall Cavendish International (Asia): 131 • Giles Massot/Asimages: 66, 86, 94, 104 • The Netherlands Ministry of Foreign Affairs: 7, 8, 24, 33, 34, 36, 42, 47, 72, 97, 99, 105 • Christine Osborne: 12, 21, 22, 35, 37, 39, 60, 73, 81, 103, 123 • Panos Pictures: 9, 49, 53, 54, 122 • Photo Bart Versteeg: 57, 93, 107, 111 • F. Roos: 68 • Bob Seward: 10, 11, 13, 14, 23, 27, 43, 65, 67, 74, 75, 79, 80, 84, 98, 101, 102, 118, 119, 125 • David Simson: 15, 41, 76, 92, 95, 96, 106, 109, 115, 116, 121, 124, 129 • Audrius Tomonis/www. banknotes.com: 135 • TopFoto: 18

PRECEDING PAGE

Dutch children playing among tulips.

ACKNOWLEDGMENTS

Thanks to Peter Theunisson of the Netherlands Embassy in Washington, D.C., for information on Dutch towns.

Marshall Cavendish Benchmark
99 White Plains Road
Tarrytown, NY 10591
Website: www.marshallcavendish.us

© Times Editions Private Limited 1995
© Marshall Cavendish International (Asia) Private Limited 2006
All rights reserved. First edition 1995. Second edition 2006.
® "Cultures of the World" is a registered trademark of Times Publishing Limited.

Originated and designed by Times Editions
An imprint of Marshall Cavendish International (Asia) Private Limited
A member of Times Publishing Limited

Library of Congress Cataloging-in-Publication Data
Seward, Pat, 1939–
    Netherlands / by Pat Seward and Sunandini Arora Lal. – 2nd ed.
        p. cm. – (Cultures of the world)
    Summary: "Provides comprehensive information on the geography, history, governmental structure, economy,
        cultural diversity, peoples, religion, and culture of the Netherlands" – Provided by publisher.
    Includes bibliographical references and index.
    ISBN 0-7614-2052-5 (alk. paper)
    1. Netherlands – Juvenile literature. I. Arora Lal, Sunandini. II. Title. III. Series.
    DJ18.S49 2006
    949.2 — dc22   2005019823

Printed in China

7 6 5 4 3 2 1

CONTENTS

A Dutch woman from Edam
in traditional headdress.

The Netherlands has long been known as the florist of Europe. For the Dutch, bulbs and flowers, especially tulips, are major money-makers.

INTRODUCTION

THE GEOGRAPHICAL LOCATION of the Netherlands has been the decisive factor in shaping its development, the character of its people, and its culture. The country is dominated by water, having three great rivers and its eastern coastline facing the North Sea. Nearly half the area of the country is below sea level, and for centuries the Dutch have fought the sea—losing land at one point only to win it back at another. A large percentage of the land was created by the Dutch.

At the same time, the sea and rivers have presented the Dutch with trading opportunities, which they have carefully nurtured. The navigable rivers allow the Dutch to trade with other European countries, and the sea on their doorstep enables them to open trade markets around the world. Through diligent trade abroad and careful management at home, this small country has achieved a world influence out of all proportion to its size and population.

GEOGRAPHY

IN THE NETHERLANDS IT IS SAID that the Lord created the land, except for Holland, which was created by the Dutch. The history, economy, and character of the Dutch people have been strongly influenced by their continuous battle with the sea, and the rivers that flow through their low-lying land.

The country is officially known as the Netherlands, but it is often called "Holland." This name actually applies only to the two provinces of North and South Holland, which border the North Sea in the Amsterdam-The Hague area. Those who live in the Netherlands are called "the Dutch," a word which also describes their language. The name Netherlands comes from the word *neder*, meaning "low" and *lands*, meaning "countries."

The Netherlands—a little larger than Maryland and a little smaller than West Virginia—is one of the smallest countries in northern Europe. It is situated at the mouth of the Rhine River, which originates 820 miles (1,320 km) away in the Alps, and flows into the North Sea. To the east the Netherlands is bordered by Germany; and to the south, by Belgium. To the north and west is the North Sea, an ever-present force.

The Kingdom of the Netherlands also includes the Netherlands Antilles in the Caribbean. These islands include Curaçao and Bonaire in the western Leeward Islands, and St. Eustatius, Saba, and St. Maarten in the northern Leeward Islands. Aruba was part of the Netherlands Antilles until 1986, when it gained autonomous status within the Netherlands.

Above: **A dike formed by raised land. Dunes and dikes protect low-lying areas that would otherwise be flooded by the sea. Without dikes, about one-third of the land would be flooded.**

Opposite: **The Dutch are seldom far from water—be it the sea, lakes, or canals that wind through the countryside.**

DIFFERENT REGIONS

Much of the Netherlands consists of land reclaimed from the sea over the past seven or eight hundred years. About a third of the total area lies below sea level, with the lowest point, near Rotterdam, 22 feet (6.7 m) below the level of the sea. More than half the country is less than 16 feet (4.8 m) above sea level and, because of the presence of large lakes such as the IJsselmeer (EH-sul-meer), one-sixth of the country is under water.

The low-lying western coastal region is characterized by polders, dikes, canals, and lakes. A polder is an area of reclaimed land, often below sea level, inside a dike or wall constructed to keep the sea from flooding in. Polders can span many square miles in area and often contain towns and villages, in addition to large expanses of farmland. Many Dutch cities, including Amsterdam and The Hague, are built on polders.

Most of the lakes are found in the polder region. The Netherlands' largest lake is the IJsselmeer. In 1932 the Dutch dammed the Zuiderzee (ZOU-der-zay), originally an inlet of the North Sea. A 19-mile (30-km) barrier dam was built linking the provinces of North Holland and Friesland (FREES-land). Over the years, the resulting lake, the IJsselmeer, has become freshwater because of the continuous fresh water flow from the IJssel River. Friesland—a farming province with its own distinct language—lies to the north of the IJsselmeer. The southern part of the lake has been reclaimed to form a new province called Flevoland (FLAY-voh-land).

Above: **Most of the Netherlands' landscape is totally flat. About 40 percent of the Netherlands' land area consists of polders. The polder region is also the country's main farming region. Canals drain the polder region.**

Opposite: **Aerial view of Flevoland.**

Over many centuries, sand deposited by the sea has built up dunes along the coastline, resulting in the string of low-lying Frisian Islands. These enclose the Waddenzee (WAH-den-zay)—another inlet of the North Sea—and protect the coast from flooding. The waters here are seldom more than 10 feet (3 m) deep even at high tide, and it is possible to walk from the mainland to the islands across the mud flats at low tide.

Along the southwest coast, the Schelde (SGHEL-duh), Waal, and Maas rivers form a complex river delta. This delta province, Zeeland (meaning "land of the sea"), has always been vulnerable to flooding.

The inner parts of the country are at higher altitudes than the polder region so they are not threatened by flooding, but these provinces are not as well irrigated by rivers. Inland areas, such as the Limburg Province and the region along the German border, have poor soil and low hills. The highest point, Vaalser, at 1,053 feet (322 m), is in the far southeast where the Dutch, German, and Belgian borders meet.

THE POWER IN THE WIND

Were it not for the windmill, the Netherlands as we know it would not exist today. For more than 600 years, the Dutch have used windmills to drain their land and keep it dry. Wherever one looks, there are windmills of one kind or another: small meadow mills in the fields, mills standing on artificial hills, mills with external stages or balconies, brick mills, wooden mills, and thatched mills. It is almost impossible to travel any significant distance without seeing either the chunky traditional mill with its broad sails, or its modern descendant—the tall wind turbine with its shining blades spinning in the breeze.

Although they were primarily used for drainage during their height of popularity, windmills also performed many other tasks. Initially they were developed for grinding grain such as wheat and corn, then spices, paint, and flint for pottery. In 1592 Cornelis Cornelisz built the first wind-

powered sawmill. Other types of mills were developed for creating wood pulp used for paper, for the extraction of linseed and rapeseed oil, and for pounding hemp.

The earliest mills were post mills, in which all the moving parts—the sails, the gearing, and the millstones—were contained in a hut-like structure that turned on a central vertical post. Interior wooden gears (*left*) turned the sails. Access to the cramped interior was by means of a short ladder at the rear of the mill. Generally, post mills and their close relatives, the wip mills—with their rectangular mill houses and pyramid-shaped bases—were quite small. Their size tended to limit their uses to grinding corn and pumping water. Nevertheless, they were constructed in the hundreds, and they can still be seen in significant numbers today.

Since windmills were such a visible and important part of the landscape, they were also used for sending messages. Sails that were set at vertical or horizontal meant that the mill was ready to start work; if the sails were at 45 degrees to the ground, the windmill could not work. News of a birth was signaled by the vertical sails being stopped just before reaching the highest point; deaths were signaled by sails stopped just after the highest point. On special occasions, the sails were decorated with baskets, tin hearts, garlands of flowers, and angels.

Windmills have their own names, which can be seen painted on the head, just below the point where the sails are attached. A visitor might see "Goliath," with "The Four Winds" and "de Jonge Hendrik" a little farther on. The parchment on which the 1776 Declaration of Independence was written came from a windmill called "Dee Schoolmeester." The English word "gang" is said to come from a Dutch word meaning a group of windmills working together.

The days when the windmill played an active role in Dutch life have long since passed. By the end of World War I, the windmill as a serious source of industrial power had ended. At one time, the Netherlands could boast between nine and ten thousand active windmills, but their small capacity, their vulnerability to fire and wind damage, and the increasing availability of better sources of power meant that they could not survive. In recent times, their function has been taken over by the electric motor and the electric pump.

Barely 1,000 windmills remain, but they are popular tourist attractions throughout the Dutch countryside and the towns. One of the major sights of the Rotterdam area, for instance, is the complex of large drainage mills along the Kinderdijk (KIN-der-dayk) (*below*). Today many replicas and models of windmills are found in the gardens of suburban homes.

Once polders are developed, they are turned over to agriculture, and towns and villages are established nearby. This is reclaimed land in the former Zuiderzee.

RECLAIMING THE LAND

Land reclamation takes place in distinct stages. First, dikes are built around the area to be reclaimed. Then, water in the enclosed area is pumped out until dry land—the polder—starts to appear. To keep the polder dry, a network of small canals is constructed to drain the water into collector canals. From here the water is pumped to canals outside and above the polder, to be carried to sea. As rain, sea, or river water continually seeps into the polder, pumping is maintained daily.

Even after the polder's surface has dried, it is still unsuitable for agriculture due to the salt residue left by the sea. Coarse grass is planted and left to grow for a few years; this slowly eliminates the salt and helps to bind the soil together. Rain and continuous pumping further remove all traces of salt. Finally, the land is turned over to agriculture and settlement.

One of the largest reclamation projects occurred in 1932 after the damming of the Zuiderzee. Once this was turned into a large inland lake, four large polders were reclaimed and drained: the Wieringermeer, the North-East, South, and East Flevoland polders. These four polders have increased the country's land area by about 407,000 acres (165,000 hectares), nearly 5 percent of the country's total land area.

THE GREAT STORM OF 1953

The Netherlands is especially vulnerable to flooding by the sea. This poses a real danger to its people, 60 percent of whom live in low-lying regions. Although the many canals, dams, dikes, and pumping stations work around the clock to prevent flooding, they are not always effective.

On the night of January 31, 1953, a disastrous storm, combined with high tides and gale force winds, brought the North Sea sweeping over the sea defenses. The notorious North Sea surge breached dikes and barriers, and swept over the entire province of Zeeland and large parts of North Brabant and South Holland. Over 1,800 people drowned, along with tens of thousands of farm animals. More than 130 towns were destroyed and almost 50,000 homes were flooded.

Damage to buildings and land ran into hundreds of millions of Dutch guilders. About 400,000 acres (162,000 hectares) of land was flooded. Hard-won agricultural land was contaminated by salt, large areas of the southwest disappeared under the waves, and the sea water even reached Rotterdam's suburbs, about 25 miles (40 km) inland.

THE DELTA PROJECT

The Delta Project in Zeeland Province was devised to prevent any further disasters like the 1953 flood. The plan envisaged the construction of a series of dams where the Rhine and Schelde rivers open into the sea, connecting the low islands facing the North Sea to create a barrier between the coastline and the sea.

Three artificial islands were constructed on existing sandbanks to shield the estuaries from the sea. However, many people objected to the enclosure of what they regarded as a unique and beautiful area, and there was also pressure to allow commercial fishing to continue. Eventually an open dam or storm-surge barrier was built across the Eastern Schelde—2 miles (3.2 km) long with 65 concrete piers, between which 62 steel gates are suspended. These vertical gates can be lowered to keep out floodwater. Dams and secondary dikes were also built in other parts of Zeeland Province.

In this low-lying land, high tides and strong winds are a constant threat and have broken flood barriers, causing serious loss of life and land. This is the storm-surge barrier in Eastern Schelde, Zeeland.

During springtime Blue-bells bloom.

CLIMATE

The climate in the Netherlands is typical of coastal northern Europe—mild, wet, and cool. Although the Netherlands is part of the European mainland, the Gulf Stream and the westerly sea winds protect the country from the extremes of the central European winter.

Average rainfall is evenly spread over the year at 30 inches (76 cm). Temperatures rarely reach extremes of either heat or cold, although average temperatures in Europe have gradually risen over the past 200 years. Amsterdam's average winter temperature in January is about 41°F (5°C). Summer temperatures in July hover around 69°F (21°C).

There is little variation in climate from one region to another, although maritime effects are less noticeable farther inland. The mild, damp climate supports grasslands and livestock farming, and favors horticulture.

Mild winters mean that shipping is seldom icebound. On the other hand, frequent changes in weather—another result of being close to the North Sea—often give rise to fog and slippery road conditions in winter. The flat areas of North and South Holland facing the North Sea are very windy, and as a result, wind turbines produce significant amounts of electricity and are frequently sited in this region.

FLORA AND FAUNA

The Netherlands is such a crowded country that wildlife has to fit in wherever it can. Wildlife mainly takes the form of birds, fish, and small, rather than large, animals.

Special areas have been created to protect flowers and trees, wildlife, and natural habitats. Hawks, cormorants, swans, ducks, and geese abound in these sanctuaries, as do small mammals such as squirrels. In addition, wading birds can be found in large numbers on the mud-flats at the mouths of the many rivers. Foxes, boar, red deer, and the dormouse are found in the higher provinces.

The grey heron is a wading bird that is found in mudflats near polders and estuarine regions.

Land reclamation and the construction of dams have had an adverse effect on birds, marine creatures, and coastal flora. Most early dams were solid, except for a few with locks to serve coastal shipping. Although solid dams were effective in protecting the coastline, they had certain disadvantages, especially for species of birds that depended for their food on the continual covering and uncovering of mud banks formed by the tide. In addition the dammed lakes slowly lost their salt content, posing a potential threat to the well-being of both the oyster population and the fishermen who depended on them for their living.

As time passed, however, it became apparent that oysters were able to cope with the tideless conditions. And when the wading birds left, other birds, notably flamingos, moved in to take their place. Nature has adapted to the new conditions, but the Dutch authorities still receive complaints from environmentalists about the long- and short-term effects of the dams.

TOWNS AND SETTLEMENTS

The densest concentration of population in the Netherlands is found in the Randstad (ROHN-stadt, meaning Rim City) area. This stretches from Amsterdam to Rotterdam and includes the towns of Haarlem, Leiden, The Hague, and Utrecht (OOH-trekht).

AMSTERDAM Amsterdam, the capital of the Netherlands, straddles the IJ and Amstel rivers and is named after a dam on the Amstel River. This city of 745,000 residents is surrounded by a network of canals and encircled by tall, elegant buildings. In the 16th century, Amsterdam became the center of economic prosperity in the Netherlands and, in the 19th century, it also became the diamond center of the world.

Schiphol (SHIP-hol) Airport, south of the city, is one of the most important hub airports in Europe. The tourist industry has added to Amsterdam's importance. Events such as film festivals, flower parades, and outdoor concerts are some of the attractions for tourists as well as locals looking for entertainment.

Among Amsterdam's most famous features are its *grachtengordel* (GRACH-ten-GHOR-del), three canals that fan out in a concentric circle: the Herengracht, the Keizersgracht, and the Prinsengracht.

THE HAGUE Although it is not the capital of the Netherlands, the government and administration of the country is in The Hague. The city's official name is 'S Gravenhage (SGRAH-ven-HAH-geh), but it is commonly called Den Haag (dun HAAGH) by the Dutch. International organizations such as the International Court of Justice (part of the United Nations) and the International Institute of Social Studies are located in The Hague, which has a population of 476,000.

ROTTERDAM   Rotterdam is the second largest city in the Netherlands and the world's largest port. It lies on the Nieuwe Maas River about 19 miles (30 km) from the North Sea, and has a population of 603,000. Rotterdam is connected to the industrial heartland of Europe by an extensive system of canals linked to the Rhine River.

During World War II, Rotterdam was almost completely destroyed by both German and Allied bombing raids, but it has since been fully rebuilt.

UTRECHT   The fourth largest city in the Netherlands, Utrecht is an ancient city dating back to Roman times. The city's university was founded in 1636 and is the second oldest in the country. The Old Canal flows through the city center well below street level. Utrecht's industries produce a variety of manufactured goods. It has a population of 267,000.

MAASTRICHT   Maastricht was initially a Roman town guarding an important crossing of the Maas River. Due to its proximity to Belgium and Germany, it is a cosmopolitan city with its own dialect, a diverse architectural style, and a rich international cuisine. Maastricht is largely Catholic, in contrast to the Protestant north. Today, the town is an important trading and industrial center specializing in ceramics, paper-making, and cement. It has a population of 122,000.

HISTORY

THE HISTORY OF THE NETHERLANDS has been connected with that of its neighbors, Belgium and Luxembourg, for the past 2,000 years. For many centuries, these three countries were known collectively as the Low Countries.

FOREIGN INVASIONS

Lacking mountains and other such natural borders, the Netherlands has been invaded and occupied by foreign powers for much of its history. From the first to the fourth centuries, the Romans occupied the Low Countries, including Celtic tribes such as the Batavi and the Frisians. The Frisians are believed to have pioneered the building of dikes. Over 2,000 years ago, they built mounds of earth along the marshy coast of Friesland to keep the sea out. Sometimes, by piercing the dikes and flooding the land, water was used to keep the enemy out.

From the fifth century onward, the Germanic Saxons and Franks occupied most of the country, except for the lands held by the Frisians. In the eighth century, Charlemagne, a Frankish king, incorporated the Low Countries into his Holy Roman Empire, and in the ninth century, Vikings from Scandinavia made the Utrecht area one of their bases.

Between the 10th and 13th centuries, present-day provinces were carved out and stabilized by a succession of princes, bishops, and counts. From the 14th to the 16th centuries, the Low Countries came under a succession of foreign rulers—the French Burgundians, the Austrian Hapsburgs, and the Spanish.

Above: **A coat of arms at Kasteeltuinen in Arcen, a town in Limburg.**

Opposite: **A replica of the *Amsterdam* sailing ship at the Maritime Museum. The ship sank on her maiden voyage in 1749. The period marked the golden age for Dutch naval explorations.**

Ruins at Valkenburg Castle in Limburg Province date back almost 1,000 years.

THE MIDDLE AGES

During the Middle Ages, the area now known as the Netherlands was split into several autonomous duchies and counties in addition to land ruled by the Bishop of Utrecht. The French Burgundians controlled northern France and what is now Belgium. Their power expanded to the present-day provinces of Limburg and North Brabant in the late 14th century. In the 15th century, this was extended to Holland, Zeeland, and Gelderland.

In 1477, Mary, daughter and heir of the duke of Burgundy, married into the Hapsburg family of Austria, and as a result the Low Countries came under Hapsburg control. Mary's son, Philip, later married into the Spanish royal family, and Philip's son, Charles, ascended the Spanish throne. In 1515, Charles I of Spain inherited the Low Countries from his father. The Low Countries were nominally Catholic, although Amsterdam was tolerant of Protestants and became the focus of much Protestant inward migration.

DUTCH REVOLT

As Protestantism spread through the largely Catholic European countries, Charles I became concerned about a possible Protestant revolt. As such, strict Catholicism was imposed on Amsterdam. In 1555, he abdicated in favor of his son, Philip II. A devout Catholic, Philip condemned thousands of Dutch Protestants to death for heresy.

He sent the Duke of Alva to strengthen Catholic control of Amsterdam in 1567. However, the Dutch did not take kindly to being given orders by Philip, a distant, foreign king who had been born and brought up in Spain. In 1568, Prince William of Orange raised an army to fight the Spanish, marking the beginning of the Eighty Years' War of independence. In addition to religious concerns, Philip also wanted to limit the rapidly expanding Dutch economy, which threatened Spanish interests.

By 1572 William had liberated Zeeland and Holland, and in 1573 he defeated the Duke of Alva's army in a battle at Zuiderzee. Although both the Dutch Catholics and Protestants joined forces to fight the Spanish, they remained divided about religion. The northern Dutch provinces were largely Protestant, while the south was mainly Catholic.

In 1581, seven northern provinces signed the Union of Utrecht treaty, under which they declared themselves the independent United Provinces of the Netherlands. The southern provinces—present-day Belgium and Luxembourg—remained under Spanish Catholic domination. However, Spain continued its land and sea attacks to regain control of the northern provinces. The Eighty Years' War came to an end in 1648, when Spain finally recognized the Netherlands' independence.

The tomb of William of Orange at Delft. Nicknamed William the Silent for his ability to be discreet, he is remembered as the father of the nation. After winning independence, William was appointed the *stadhouder*, or governor, in 1579. He was killed by the Spanish in 1584.

21

THE GOLDEN AGE

As Amsterdam became the most important commercial center in Europe, its residents constructed many imposing buildings that still survive today. This is a house in Amsterdam dating back to the 17th century.

The United Provinces controlled shipping on the Rhine River due to their location. Amsterdam began to prosper as a port, and the stage was set for Dutch adventurers to explore Asia and the Americas and to open up new areas for trade.

In the 17th century, Dutch merchants established trading posts all over the world, from the Far East to the Caribbean. The Dutch East India Company (Vereenigde Oost-Indische Compagnie or the VOC) was founded in Amsterdam in 1602 to handle trade between the United Provinces and territories in the Indian Ocean. The Dutch West India Company was established in 1621 to trade with the Americas and Africa. As commerce expanded, the United Provinces became extremely wealthy.

The newfound prosperity and religious tolerance of the Dutch sparked a flourishing spiritual and cultural life. This Golden Age produced many great Dutch painters—particularly Rembrandt van Rijn, Jan Vermeer, Frans Hals, and Jacob van Ruisdael.

In addition, the Golden Age was notable for its contributions in furniture making, gold and silversmithing, and architecture. Scientific advances were also made. Antonie van Leeuwenhoek invented the microscope and studied microbiology.

1615

BOURTANGE

Bourtange (boor-TANG-eh), in the northeastern Netherlands near the German border, is one of many fortified towns that played a vital role in protecting the United Provinces.

The town was built in 1593 on the orders of William of Orange. Its defenses included a star-shaped network of lakes and canals. At its heart was a central square, with streets that led directly to the various bastions within the protective moat. Lookouts posted on every corner gave warnings of approaching enemies.

Spanish forces besieged the town in the very year that it was built but without success. In 1672, a marauding German army captured 28 cities and entrenchments in northern Netherlands and demanded the surrender of Bourtange. The town's governor, Captain Prott, putting his trust in the surrounding marshes and in the well-tried defenses of the fortress, refused. Legend states that the Germans offered Prott 200,000 guilders to surrender, but he replied that he had an equal number of bullets for his foe. As a result of Prott's defiant response, Bourtange was attacked, but the German army eventually suffered a crushing defeat and withdrew.

CONTINUING WARS

The Netherlands' prosperity led to conflicts with other European countries—wars with the British and French, continuing struggles with Spain, and opportunist forays by the Germans.

The Dutch and British went to war twice for control of the sea. In the First Anglo-Dutch War, the Dutch Admiral van Tromp had to yield, but in 1667 Admiral de Ruyter made a daring raid into the River Medway, near London—the only time foreign guns were fired in the British capital.

The War of the Spanish Succession, where the Dutch, English, and French all laid claim to the throne of Spain, broke out at the turn of the 18th century and dragged on for 12 years. This war drained Dutch finances and led indirectly to the end of the Golden Age.

CONQUERING A WIDER WORLD

Dutch interests overseas expanded rapidly during the 17th century as explorers braved the unknown to open trading routes and new settlements. As the result of an embargo on Dutch trade with Spain and Portugal, the Dutch turned their attention to direct trade with the East.

In 1596 Cornelis de Houtman arrived in Java and established Dutch occupation in the Indonesian archipelago. Batavia (now Jakarta, capital of Indonesia) was established by Jan Pieterzoon Coen in 1619 and became the administrative center of the colony. Known as the Dutch East Indies, it remained a Dutch colony until 1949, when it became independent.

Dutch adventurers and traders explored the world in their sailing ships. In 1596 William Barents discovered Spitzbergen in the Arctic Ocean while searching for a northeast route to India. New Zealand was discovered by another Dutch sailor, Abel Tasman, who also gave his name to the island of Tasmania in Australia. The Cape Colony, now Cape Town in South Africa, was founded by Jan van Riebeek in 1652 as a stopping point on the route to India.

In South America, the Guinea coast was occupied by the Dutch in 1613. Ten years later, parts of Brazil also became a Dutch colony. In North America, Nieuw Amsterdam was founded in 1625, and 20 years later Peter Stuyvesant became its last Dutch governor. By 1634, the Dutch also had a string of small possessions in the Antilles in the eastern Caribbean, many of which are still part of the Netherlands Antilles today.

FRENCH REVOLUTION AND AFTER

The Dutch remained independent for 150 years, until the rise of the French Empire in Napoleonic times. After a French army occupied the United Provinces in 1795, the conquered territory was renamed the Batavian Republic and became a vassal state of the French Empire. In 1806, Napoleon installed his brother Louis as king of Holland, and in 1810 the country was annexed to France.

The French occupation ended in 1814 when the Kingdom of the Netherlands declared independence. The new country united the present-day Netherlands, Belgium, and Luxembourg. Unlike the previous republican system, where a *stadhouder,* or governor, ruled the country, it became a constitutional monarchy. The Netherlands invited former stadhouder William IV, a descendant of Prince William of Orange, to return from exile and reign over their new constitutional monarchy as King William I. During the 19th century, the parliament became stronger as the sovereign's powers were slowly curbed. In 1814, a new constitution decreed that the monarch should govern and that ministers should be accountable to the sovereign. The constitution of 1848, which is still in force today, made ministers accountable to an elected parliament.

In 1839, the southern Catholic provinces of the Netherlands gained independence and became the country of Belgium. Luxembourg became independent in 1890, when Wilhelmina became queen of the Netherlands. Due to an ancient law that prevented women from ruling the grand duchy, Luxembourg could not recognize Wilhelmina as the monarch and ended its union with the Netherlands.

A statue of Queen Wilhelmina. The queen was a keen ruler who also had a shrewd mind for investment. She was the first woman to exceed a personal net worth of over a billion dollars.

WORLD WARS AND GERMAN OCCUPATION

A monument in Dam Square, Amsterdam, commemorating Dutch victims of World War II.

Located between Britain and Germany—opposing countries in World War I—the Netherlands was able to maintain its neutrality during the war. However, during World War II, the Netherlands was invaded by Germany in May 1940. After the bombing of Rotterdam, the Dutch capitulated in the face of Germany's overwhelming military power. Queen Wilhelmina and the Dutch government set up a government-in-exile in England, and her daughter, Princess Juliana, went to Canada with her family for safety.

German occupation of the Netherlands lasted five years and inflicted misery, humiliation, and degradation on the population. Food shortages, lack of freedom, forced labor, censorship, and curfews were common. The deportation of Dutch Jews to concentration camps deprived the country of a well-integrated and vigorous minority. A Dutch resistance movement soon sprang up, but the Germans retaliated with random killings after each act of defiance.

Unfortunately for the Dutch, a bold plan by the Allies to bring the war to a swift end in September 1944 failed. The "Bridge Too Far" operation—a plan to capture the Arnhem bridge over the Rhine and isolate German troops—was a disaster. In the terrible winter that followed, thousands of Dutch died of starvation. Many were reduced to eating tulip bulbs to survive.

By the end of the German occupation, Dutch cities were in shambles, the economy was in ruins, and the population was starving. In April 1945, the Allies liberated the Netherlands, and food and other supplies poured in to relieve the suffering. Queen Wilhelmina and her government-in-exile returned to pick up the pieces and started the long task of reconstruction.

END OF EMPIRE

Until World War II, the Netherlands held colonies in Southeast Asia, the Caribbean, and South America, but these territories sought independence after 1945. After fierce fighting, the Netherlands was forced in 1949 to recognize the independence of its colonies in Southeast Asia, which later formed the Republic of Indonesia. By the 1954 Charter for the Kingdom, Surinam and the Netherlands Antilles (Aruba, Curaçao, Bonaire, St. Eustatius, Saba, and St. Maarten) in the eastern Caribbean became partners with the Netherlands, although the Netherlands remained responsible for defense and foreign policy. Surinam became independent in 1975, while the Netherlands Antilles have full autonomy in its internal affairs, and have their own head of government and cabinet.

The tombstone of a Dutch colonialist in Malacca, Malaysia, dating back to 1656. The Dutch captured Malacca from the Portuguese in 1641 and governed it until 1824.

THE NETHERLANDS TODAY

Dependence on international trade has led the Dutch to take a particular interest in international law. Many international treaties are signed here and the International Court of Justice is located in The Hague. The Netherlands is also part of many international organizations. These include the European Union, the United Nations, the North Atlantic Treaty Organization, the Organization for Economic Cooperation and Development, and the Benelux Customs Union (together with Belgium and Luxembourg). Dutch support for disarmament, human rights, and the elimination of racial discrimination is widely respected.

During the 1990s the Netherlands was a major force for the economic and political unification of Europe. However, recent political upheavals—such as the assassination of politician Pim Fortuyn in 2002, who was known for his controversial views on immigration and Islam—have somewhat tarnished the impression of Dutch commitment to freedom of opinion. In October 2005, suspects were detained in various Dutch cities for allegedly planning terror attacks.

International Court of Justice at the Peace Palace in The Hague.

THE EUROPEAN UNION

The Netherlands is a founding member of the European Union (EU), which began as the European Economic Community (EEC). The EEC was set up in 1958 to facilitate the free trade of goods and services among member countries. Initially there were six members—Belgium, West Germany, France, Italy, Luxembourg, and the Netherlands. By 2005, membership of the union increased to 25 countries, with Romania and Bulgaria expected to join in 2007, and Croatia and Turkey later in the decade.

In late 1991, when the Netherlands held the presidency of the then EEC, it promoted the Maastricht Treaty, which promoted the evolution of a supranational federal Europe, including full monetary union with a common currency and the removal of all trade barriers. The Maastricht Treaty created the European Union, which incorporated the European Coal and Steel Community, the European Atomic Energy Commission, and the EEC. The European Union came into being on November 1, 1993 and is, in effect, an enlarged and more powerful EEC with a common foreign and security policy and an agreement to cooperate on justice and home affairs issues. Euro currency bills and coins were introduced into general circulation in 2002 and are accepted in several EU countries. If all EU countries approve, the EU Constitution will be established in 2006.

The Binnenhof complex in The Hague is the center of the Dutch government.

GOVERNMENT

THE NETHERLANDS IS A REPUBLIC with a constitutional monarchy. Although most Dutch people are fiercely democratic in outlook, the country has a widely respected hereditary monarchy.

PARLIAMENT

The Dutch parliament is called the States General, a term left over from feudal times, when representatives of various estates were summoned by their lords to discuss political and financial matters. The States General has two chambers—a Lower and an Upper House.

The Lower House has 150 members who are directly elected by the population for a four-year term. Universal male suffrage was introduced in 1917. Women were given the vote two years later, and until 1970 voting in a general election was compulsory by law.

The Upper House has 75 members elected by provincial councils for a four-year term. These councils are also elected by universal suffrage, so both houses have virtually the same political composition. The States General, the queen, and the ministers form the legislature.

Legislation is introduced by the executive branch to the Lower House, which can amend a bill or refuse to pass it. The Lower House may also introduce legislation, although this right is seldom exercised. Legislation passed by the Lower House goes to the Upper House, which can vote on bills but may not amend them. When a bill has passed through both houses, it goes to the monarch for assent. It becomes law only when it is signed by both the monarch and the responsible minister.

Above: **An aerial view of the Binnenhof at The Hague. The Binnenhof has been the home of the Dutch parliament since the 1500s.**

Opposite: **The façade of an old town hall in Arnhem.**

31

THE EXECUTIVE

After an election, the monarch appoints ministers on the recommendation of a *formateur* (form-a-TERH), who sometimes becomes the prime minister. The parties forming the new government divide the cabinet posts between them based on the number of seats they have in parliament. Ministers are not members of parliament; they have the right to speak in the States General, but not to vote.

The complex of the Lower House of the States General.

The prime minister and other ministers form the cabinet and coordinate government policy. From 1994 to 2002, Wim Kok of the Labor Party was the prime minister. After the general election of 2002, a new coalition government was formed from an alliance of three political parties. The current prime minister is Jan Peter Balkenende of the Christian Democratic Appeal.

THE MONARCHY

The Dutch monarchy belongs to the House of Orange Nassau, which dates back to the 16th century. Its founder was Prince William of Orange.

In 1890 there was no male heir, so the throne passed to the monarch's eldest daughter, Wilhelmina. Since then, the Netherlands has had two additional queens—Juliana became queen when Wilhelmina abdicated in 1948, and the present Queen Beatrix succeeded to the throne when Juliana abdicated in 1980. Queen Beatrix's eldest son, William Alexander, is the crown prince. In a political scene dominated by shifting alliances created by the system of proportional representation, the sovereign is the one fixed factor. The monarchy can, however, be abolished by an Act of Parliament. The Dutch would probably declare a republic if the House of Orange died out.

ATTITUDES TOWARD ROYALTY

Before her marriage, Queen Beatrix studied at Leiden University. Her marriage to the German Prince Claus von Amsberg was not popular with the older Dutch generation, who remembered the German occupation in World War II. Happily, the queen has endeared herself to the public by her egalitarianism and her conscientious dedication to her role in the national life. Although Queen Beatrix is one of the wealthiest women in Europe, lavish display of wealth is definitely not the style of the Dutch monarchy. The family is admired because its members live much like ordinary citizens. The Royal Palace in Amsterdam, for example, is used only for official functions. The queen's home is not a palace but a house called Huis den Bosch (HOUSE den bosh, or the House in the Woods) near The Hague.

Affection for the monarchy, however, does not mean that it is above criticism. In the 1970s, when Prince Bernhard, Queen Juliana's husband, was implicated in a business scandal, he had to withdraw from public life.

Queen Beatrix and Prince Claus. The monarch's role today is mainly ceremonial. One of the most important state occasions is the opening of parliament by the queen on the third Tuesday of September each year at the *Ridderzaal* (REE-der-zhal), or Hall of Knights. Prince Claus died in October 2002.

PROPORTIONAL REPRESENTATION

Many countries, such as the United States and the United Kingdom, have an electoral system whereby the candidate with the most votes wins the election. However, this "winner takes all" system is not used in the Netherlands. Instead, a system of proportional representation is used.

It is often argued that proportional representation allows for public opinion to be more fairly represented. In the Netherlands, parliamentary seats are allocated to a political party in proportion to the votes it receives.

Elections to the Lower House of the States General (*right*) are based on proportional representation among the various political parties. There are about 40 political parties in the Netherlands, and since no single party has been able to command a majority of votes, governments are almost always coalitions. Since consensus government is a long tradition with the Dutch, coalition governments are able to work together in the interest of the nation.

OTHER INSTITUTIONS

Three other government institutions—the Council of State, the General Chamber of Audit, and the National Ombudsman—play an important part in Dutch public life.

The Council of State consists of the queen as president of the council, a vice president responsible for the daily operations of the council, the crown prince, and 28 members appointed for life. Members whose terms of office are indefinite are chosen for their experience in administrative matters. The Council is the highest advisory body in the state and must be consulted before any legislation goes to the States General.

The General Chamber of Audit has three members and their deputies. It monitors the management of state funds. The Chamber submits an annual report to the queen and the Lower House, and this is made available to the public. Members are appointed for life, and they retire when they reach the age of 70.

An anti-government demonstration that was held in Amsterdam.

In 1982 the Dutch government created the post of National Ombudsman. The word *ombudsman* (ohm-BOODS-mahn) is of Swedish origin and means an investigator of public complaints. Accordingly, the Dutch ombudsman is an independent officer who investigates complaints made by members of the public against the executive branch. The ombudsman has wide-ranging powers to examine any aspect of the relationship of the government to the ordinary citizen.

CHECKS AND BALANCES

As with all modern democracies, the government of the Netherlands has a system of checks and balances to ensure that political power is exercised according to the law. The government is responsible to the people through their elected representatives in the States General.

The States General has three ways of checking the power of the government: First, it has the right to set a budget; second, it can set up independent inquiries on government matters; and finally, it has the right to question ministers and state secretaries about present or future policies.

PROVINCIAL GOVERNMENT

The country is divided into 12 provinces, each administered by a provincial council directly elected by residents of the province. Elections are held every four years under the system of proportional representation. The most densely populated province of South Holland has 83 members in its council, while Flevoland and Zeeland have the smallest councils, with 47 members each.

Council members elect a provincial executive from among themselves to handle day-to-day administration in the province. The chair of both the council and the executive board is called the Queen's Commissioner and is appointed by the Crown. The council chooses which of its members will represent the province in the Upper House of the States General.

The Delft Town Hall, heart of one of the Netherlands' more than 640 municipalities.

MUNICIPALITIES AND REGIONAL AUTHORITIES

Each town and village in the country has a municipal council. Council members are elected by proportional representation every four years. The largest municipal council has 45 members, and the smallest has only seven. Daily administration is the responsibility of the burgomaster (or mayor) and the aldermen. The burgomaster is appointed for six years by the queen on the recommendation of the government, and aldermen are elected from among the members of the municipal council.

In recent years, municipalities have found it increasingly beneficial to join forces in tackling common problems related to zoning, transportation, and the environment.

Police officers on duty at Dam Square, Amsterdam.

WATER CONTROL BOARDS

Water control boards, or *waterschappen* (WAH-ter-sghap-pen), are among the oldest democratic institutions in the Netherlands. They are responsible for managing water in the polders, and their tasks also include the construction and maintenance of roads, bridges, and other public works. Their prime role is the prevention of flooding.

Members of water boards are elected by property owners of the area in question. The most important boards are those near the sea, the major rivers, and the IJsselmeer.

THE COURTS

The Dutch legal system is relatively straightforward, and great emphasis is put on speed, simplicity, and the independence of judicial officials. Besides the subdistrict courts, district courts, courts of appeal, and the Supreme Court, specialized administrative tribunals also deal with social insurance, civil service, and other social and welfare matters. All court decisions are made by judges. The Supreme Court is responsible for deciding if the law has been properly applied.

ECONOMY

THE NETHERLANDS IS A HIGHLY INDUSTRIALIZED nation, with an open, mixed economy and one of the best credit ratings in Europe. From the late 1980s to 1991, the country experienced rapid economic growth and virtually no inflation. However, the economy has been affected by the global recession of the early 1990s, the terrorist attacks on the United States on September 11, 2001, and the war in Iraq.

The Netherlands' natural resources—agricultural land, oil, and gas—are relatively limited. However, its location has made it one of Europe's great trading nations. Entrepot trade—trade based on the transit of goods between Europe and the rest of the world—accounts for over half of the country's national income. Most of this trade goes through Rotterdam's Europoort, one of the busiest ports in the world.

However, the Netherlands' largest income generators are its industries. Agriculture is intensive in the dairy and arable sectors and in horticulture, but it accounts for a relatively small percentage of the national income.

Opposite: **An oil rig in the North Sea. In 1993, the Netherlands produced 105 million cubic feet (3 million cubic meters) of oil.**

DIAMOND CENTER OF THE WORLD

Diamond cutting has been practiced in Amsterdam since the 16th century. The first resident diamond polisher was recorded in an Amsterdam marriage register in 1586.

Since the 19th century, Amsterdam has been known as the diamond center of the world. It was here that some of the world's largest and most famous diamonds were cut and polished—the Cullinan and the Koh-i-Nohr.

Today Amsterdam produces 80 percent of the

world's industrial diamonds, used for abrasive applications such as cutting tools and drills. A smaller proportion of diamonds are sold as gems. In this photo, a diamond polisher practices his trade.

TRADE

With its ten seaports, six airports, 3,000 inland vessels, 7,500 road transportation companies, and extensive railway system, the Netherlands has been called the "Gateway to Europe." More than one-third of all seaborne goods loaded or unloaded in European Union countries pass through the Netherlands.

Two-thirds of the Netherlands' trade is with European Union countries, mainly Germany, Belgium, France, and the United Kingdom. Industrial goods make up 70 percent of exports. Major exports include machinery and transportation equipment (accounting for nearly one-fourth of the total), food and chemicals (together accounting for one-third), energy, and metals. Major imports are machinery and electrical equipment, food,

Europoort—a vast, sprawling expanse of quays, warehouses, and docks—lies downstream from Rotterdam, extending out to the Hook of Holland. Built between 1958 and 1975, the huge port covers an area of 8,900 acres (3,560 hectares). Some docks can accept ships drawing as much as 72 feet (22 m) of water. There are also five oil refineries with facilities for ocean-going tankers of up to 350,000 tons (315,000 metric tons).

beverages, tobacco, manufactured goods, transportation equipment, and energy.

The bulk of the Netherlands' trade goes through Rotterdam. Lying at the mouth of the Rhine's tributary, Rotterdam's Europoort is the largest human-made harbor and port complex in the world, extending for 21 miles (35 kilometers) from the city to the Hook of Holland.

TRANSPORTATION

The Netherlands has had an extensive canal system to transport goods and passengers for hundreds of years. The canal system, much widened and modernized, still handles a large volume of heavy goods—cargo can be transported along canals and rivers within the country and as far inland as Germany and Switzerland. Dutch carriers account for about half the international transport by water within the European Union. Most cargo goes by way of the Rhine River.

On the roads, Dutch haulers handle about one-third of international road freight within the European Union. In the air, the Royal Dutch Airlines (or KLM) is one of the best-known airlines in the world. The Netherlands' aircraft manufacturer—Fokker—produces mainly civil transport and small regional aircraft. It was taken in 1996 over by another Dutch company, Stork Aerospace, to form Stork Fokker.

The Netherlands controls a large share of Europe's shipping due to its location on the North Sea and on the estuaries of three major rivers— the Rhine, the Maas, and the Schelde.

TECHNOLOGY AND MANUFACTURING

Most industries are concentrated in urban centers, such as Amsterdam, Utrecht, Haarlem, Rotterdam, and The Hague. Manufactured products include textiles, synthetic fibers, chemicals, and metal products. Other important industries include transportation, agri-industrial products, petroleum products, and rubber. Since the Netherlands is an important shipping nation, shipbuilding is a key industry.

In electronics, Philips of Eindhoven is a multinational company that is world famous for manufacturing electrical and electronic products. Unilever is another well-known Dutch company producing foods and detergents. The Royal Dutch/Shell group is one of the world's largest oil- and gas-producing companies and is also based in the Netherlands.

In recent years the government has placed special emphasis on developing technology-related industries, such as electronics (*right*), biotechnology, computer products, and new materials production.

ENERGY

The Netherlands has extensive oil and gas fields—nearly 22,000 square miles (57,000 sq km) in the North Sea—and is a leading producer of natural gas. Natural gas production in 2001 was 2.75 trillion cubic feet (77.75 billion cubic meters) from mainland and offshore fields.

Although natural gas is used to produce electricity in 95 percent of all homes, over half of gas production is exported. However, the Netherlands' oil reserves are much smaller. Dutch oil wells supply 20 percent of domestic requirements, and the remainder has to be imported.

Since 1973 the government has followed a policy designed to reduce dependence on imported supplies. Intensive energy-saving campaigns have been conducted, and steps have been taken to develop alternative sources of power based on environment-friendly sources such as the wind. The Dutch had two nuclear power plants, but due to concerns over nuclear waste, one was shut down in 1997. The other is scheduled to cease operations in 2013.

In 1973 the global oil crisis led to an increasing interest in developing alternative sources of power. This event, along with environmental concerns, has stimulated the Dutch to develop wind turbines for generating electricity. Electricity generated by wind is not cheap, and there are concerns over noise pollution as well as hazards to birds caused by wind turbines. Nonetheless the technology holds great potential.

Tall and slim, standing up to 650 feet (198 m) high with rotors nearly 500 feet (152 m) in diameter, wind turbines rise high above the polders of North Holland. Most have two or three propeller-like blades.

Observers standing close by are amazed by the height of wind turbines and the incredible speed with which their blades slice through the air.

The Amsterdam Stock Exchange is the oldest stock exchange in the world, with its history tracing back to 1611.

MONEY MATTERS

The Netherlands' unit of currency is the euro, which is accepted in 11 other EU countries—Austria, Belgium, Finland, France, Germany, Greece, Ireland, Italy, Luxembourg, Portugal, and Spain. It was introduced into general circulation in 2002, and the old currency of the Netherlands, the guilder, has been phased out.

The euro is divided into 100 cents. Coins are issued in denominations of 1, 2, 5, 10, 20, and 50 cents; and 1 and 2 euros. Every euro coin from all countries adopting the single currency has one side in common showing the value of the coin, and one side unique to the country in which it was minted. Dutch euro coins feature a portrait of Queen Beatrix.

Bank notes are issued in denominations of 5, 10, 20, 50, 100, 200, and 500 euros. These do not have an obvious indication of the country of issue, although this information is encoded in the serial numbers of the notes. Notes issued in the Netherlands have serial numbers beginning with the letter "P," while those from other EU countries begin with a different letter or number.

The national central banks of the 11 EU countries, together with the European Central Bank (ECB), all play a decisive role in managing the euro. The ECB and the participating national banks are known collectively as Eurosystem. Aside from the ensuring a smooth transition in the adoption of the currency, the Eurosystem also looks into monetary policies and foreign exchange and payment systems. The Dutch national bank is called De Nederlandsche Bank.

AGRICULTURE

About half the Netherlands' available land is used for agriculture—60 percent of this land is allocated to livestock farming, and another 35 percent to arable farming. The remaining 5 percent supports other forms of agriculture such as horticulture and organic farming.

Today, arable farming has become less important. The cultivation of crops such as rye and oats has declined, whereas that of corn for fodder has increased. Production of wheat, sugar beets, and potatoes has increased with larger areas under cultivation and greater yields per acre.

Dairy farming takes place mainly in the Friesland and North Holland provinces. In spite of a reduction in the number of dairy cows due to EEC quotas, improved efficiency has increased production of dairy products. With a large livestock industry—14 million pigs, 5 million cattle, and 90 million chickens—the Netherlands has an enormous manure problem. Almost 100 million tons of manure have to be disposed of every year. Half is used for fertilizer, while the remaining 50 million tons are left to seep into the ground, reducing land fertility and poisoning groundwater as a consequence. This unfortunate problem has yet to be resolved.

The proportion of people working in agriculture has fallen to just 5 percent of the work force. Most farms are small—averaging about 25 acres (10 hectares)—but they are highly mechanized and efficient in labor and land use.

Most agricultural output is exported, producing a trade balance of over 7 billion dollars. Although the Netherlands produces only 1 percent of the world's dairy output, it is the world's largest exporter of dairy products. Although the number of cattle farms in the country has declined by half in the last twenty years, Dutch dairy products—made with imports from other countries—continue to rise.

The Netherlands is the third largest agricultural exporter in the world after the United States and France. The Dutch have gained 16 percent of the world dairy produce market, which includes 27 percent of the global cheese market and 60 percent of the condensed milk market.

Tulips are grown mainly in North Holland, especially from north of Leiden to south of Haarlem. When the bulbs are in bloom, the fields draw thousands of tourists who come to view the brilliant strips of color stretching across the landscape as far as the eye can see.

FLOWERSHOP OF THE WORLD

Usually cultivated under glass in the Westland area between the Hook of Holland, The Hague, and Rotterdam, most of the Netherlands' flowers are exported to the European Union.

In this "Glass City," as the Westland area is called, greenhouses extend for over 23,000 acres (9,000 hectares). Flowers are grown in gravel that is frequently flooded with water highly enriched with organic nutrients. Computers automatically regulate temperature and light by opening and closing vents and shutters in the roof and by switching on lights at night if necessary. They also control the water and nutrient supplies. Plants can be grown here year round.

Outdoor horticultural production concentrates on cultivating a variety of bulbs—tulips, daffodils, hyacinths, crocuses, and other species. The flowers and plants are sold daily at large flower auctions. One of the

TULIPS

Tulips are thought to have originated in Asia. They were brought to Europe from Turkey in the mid-16th century and were cultivated in the western parts of the Netherlands.

In the 1630s the rising demand for bulbs and the difficulties of obtaining flowers of consistent color and shape prompted a wave of wild speculation. This "tulip mania" saw prices rise dramatically, and family fortunes were both made and destroyed in the frantic trading that took place. At one point, a single white Semper Augustus bulb was sold for the equivalent of $5,000. After the bubble burst, prices returned to sensible levels.

most famous flower auctions takes place at Aalsmeer. More than 20 million cut flowers are sold here everyday.

Growers load their flowers onto trolleys, which are linked together on an automatic rail system. As each trolley enters into the auction room, a large clock on the wall is set in motion. The hand begins at a figure indicating a starting price, which is lowered as the clock hand moves round. Buyers sit at

Over two billion cut flowers and potted plants are sold at the Aalsmeer flower auction every year, many of which are exported.

their desks with fingers poised ready to press a button that will stop the clock at a price they are prepared to pay. This requires experience and quick reactions—pressing the button too early could commit buyers to too high a price, whereas pressing it too late would mean losing the flowers.

FISHING

Considering the length of the Netherlands' coastline, fishing plays a small part in the country's economy. This is due largely to over-fishing in the North Sea, land reclamation, and flood prevention schemes that have cut off once-busy ports from the open sea. Even the freshwater fishing industry has declined, and famous fishing towns, such as Volendam and Marken, have come to rely on tourism rather than fishing.

ENVIRONMENT

THE NETHERLANDS IS THE MOST densely populated country in the European Union. As the population density in towns and cities increases, there is greater pressure on the land and natural resources. More than half the land in the country is reclaimed land, or polders.

With rising population pressures and increasing industrialization and urbanization, there is a greater consumption of energy; industrial wastes pollute the land and water; and the air is contaminated, mainly from harmful industrial emissions.

ECOSYSTEMS

As in other developed nations, the road to modernization in the Netherlands has been marked by a widespread destruction of forests and other natural habitats. At the beginning of the 20th century, 28 percent of the Netherlands' land area was forested. By the mid-1970s the figure was down to 15 percent, and in 2004 only 11 percent of the Netherlands was forested. Today the Netherlands' goal is to regrow its forests by 0.3 percent each year.

With scarce cultivable land area, farmers tried for decades to increase productivity by using excessive fertilizers and pesticides. While increasing agricultural output, this led to a tragic loss of habitats for native animal and plant species.

Alarmed by this, the Dutch government devised a policy called Natuurbeleidsplan (Nature Policy Plan) in the 1990s. It

Opposite: **Storks and other migratory birds such as gulls, terns, and herons make their annual stops in the Netherlands.**

Below: **The Dutch continue to reclaim land from the sea to meet the increasing needs of the population.**

established a national ecological network of nature preserves connected by lands acquired by the government and developed into natural habitats.

WILDLIFE

In the Netherlands wildlife exists mainly in the form of fish, birds, small land mammals, and larger mammals such as deer, wild boar, and foxes. Because of the abundance of swamps and wetlands, the Netherlands has traditionally been a haven for birds.

The osprey, a migratory bird of prey, is one species that is observed more frequently today than it had been in the recent past. Ospreys are attracted to the Oostvaardersplassen, an expansive marsh in the center of the country. It has shallow water with plentiful fish, and the public is not allowed to enter most of the area so the birds may feed undisturbed.

The Waddenzee Bird Sanctuary has been developed on the island of Terschelling. Natural areas have also been established for frogs, toads, snakes, hamsters, beavers, and other small land creatures. In March and April, during the annual migration of toads during the mating season, temporary road signs are erected to alert motorists of their presence. Toads are usually shy creatures, but they come out in large numbers to migrate to the water during the mating season.

CLEANING THE AIR

The Netherlands, like several other developed countries, is under pressure to reduce its use of fossil fuels to generate energy. As a signatory to the Kyoto Protocol—a 1997 agreement among 131 nations to reduce their emissions of greenhouse gases, which have been blamed for global warming and climate change—the Netherlands is required to cut back on its emissions of carbon dioxide. However, Dutch chemical, oil, and

transportation industries consume so much energy that the emissions of carbon dioxide have actually increased in recent years.

To reduce emissions without damaging industries, European Union countries implemented a system for trading carbon dioxide emissions rights in 2005. Called the European Union Emissions Trading Scheme, it allows companies to buy and sell permits for emitting carbon dioxide. Companies are allotted permits to release a certain amount of this gas. They may either use them or sell them to other companies. This allows companies that have climate-friendly projects to sell their emissions rights to those that have a problem with emissions, allowing market forces to determine the price of cleaning the air. The European Climate Exchange is based in Amsterdam. Methane emissions are expected to come under the same rules as carbon dioxide emissions in the near future.

The Netherlands is under great pressure to reduce air pollution, particularly from the European Union, and also at home, where the high levels of emissions are preventing the further construction of housing, roads, and industrial sites.

GREEN ENERGY

The Energy Research Center of the Netherlands conducts research on the environment and energy, including wind energy, solar energy, renewable energy, and the clean burning of fossil fuels. The institute has connections to universities and other facilities in various countries, and visiting scientists from overseas collaborate on efforts to develop Earth-friendly energy sources and reduce emissions of greenhouse gases. Industries that have energy-intensive production processes can also seek advice from the institute about achieving higher energy efficiency in their operations. The institute also advises the Dutch government on environmental policies.

The Netherlands has been associated with windmills for centuries and, in fact, windmills played an important role in the creation of polders by helping to drain out the water from them. However, windmills are not a reliable energy source for modern power needs because they work only when the wind blows; when the wind does not blow, alternative sources of energy are needed.

Windmills have now been replaced by wind farms with gigantic wind turbines, but even those have a long way to go before they start generating enough consistent power to significantly supplement other modern sources of energy. In 1995 the Dutch government announced that it intended to meet 10 percent of the country's energy needs with renewable energy by the year 2020. Officials said wind energy would play an important role in this development. Although growth in this area has been below expectations, there is hope that in a few years the wind will play a more significant role in sustainable power generation.

Two nuclear power plants generated electricity for the Netherlands, but due to concerns over nuclear waste, the Dodewaard plant was shut down in 1997. The Borselle plant is scheduled to shut down in 2013.

PUBLIC EFFORTS

Residents of the Netherlands are, in general, aware of environmental issues and are diligent about recycling. They separate their garbage more precisely than do residents of the United States. Neighborhoods have communal bins where households and businesses deposit various categories of waste: paper, glass, and old clothing. Consumers are reimbursed for any plastic containers they return to the supermarket, such as beverage bottles and containers for food and other products.

Every couple of weeks, residents and businesses put out a bin containing chemical waste, ranging from batteries to cosmetics. And every week, households put out two containers of garbage, one containing "green" waste—food scraps, garden clippings, and other organic matter—and the second containing residual garbage that does not fit into any of the above categories.

In the inner city areas of Amsterdam, Rotterdam, The Hague, and Utrecht, many people prefer to ride bicycles rather than drive cars, to avoid the problems of traffic and parking. In less congested areas, too, some Dutch cycle to work or school—both for the exercise and in an attempt to be environment-friendly. More than 80 percent of the population in the Netherlands owns at least one bicycle. An increasing number of residents are driving to work, but in 2002 there were still 25 percent of residents cycling to work.

A demonstration against the drilling for gas in Waddenzee.

53

Labeled recycling bins allow people to separate their trash.

ENVIRONMENTAL ISSUES IN THE NETHERLANDS ANTILLES

The Netherlands Antilles consists of the islands of St. Maarten, Saba, St. Eustatius, Curaçao, and Bonaire in the Caribbean Sea. Oil, offshore finance, and tourism are the main industries in this area. Visitors come from all over the world to experience the natural beauty of the islands and surrounding waters, renowned for their corals and abundance of marine life.

The islands have not had effective policies for garbage recycling and reduction, and as a result there is a large volume of undisposed waste. Inadequately regulated oil production and transportation add their share of waste products. With tourism playing a major role in the islands' economy, the government of the Netherlands Antilles is understandably concerned.

The government formulated the Nature and Environment Policy Plan 2004–2007 to deal with waste, conserve natural resources, increase public awareness of environmental issues, and develop sustainable tourism in the Netherlands Antilles.

EELS

Scientists do not completely understand the life cycle of eels, many of which are found in the waters off the Netherlands. It is believed that they mature in fresh water, but they migrate to the ocean to breed. After spawning they die. The tiny offspring migrate in the opposite direction, finding their way to coastal areas.

The Dutch enjoy smoked eel, and fishermen in the Netherlands catch the fish for domestic consumption as well as for export to the Far East. Environmentalists have expressed concern over the declining eel population in recent years. They blame the decline on overfishing, ocean warming, and pollution, among other causes.

In 2004 the European Council suggested a ban on eel fishing in some areas and during some seasons, in an effort to increase the population of the fish in European coastal waters.

DUTCH

TODAY THE NETHERLANDS has a population of 16.3 million, which makes it one of the most densely populated countries in the world, with 1,246 people per square mile. In comparison, Japan has 873 people per square mile, France has 287, and the United States has only 80.

POPULATION GROWTH AND MIGRATION

The population has grown sevenfold since the first census was taken more than 150 years ago. In 1830 the Dutch numbered only 2.6 million, but improved medical care during the second half of the 19th century led to falling mortality rates and a rise in population. This growth meant that rural areas were less able to support the increasing number of people.

Up to the early 20th century, migration to towns became common. Most people moved to urban areas in North and South Holland, but after World War II, thousands of Dutch also emigrated to Canada, the United States, South Africa, Australia, and New Zealand. Later in the 1950s, as the political situation in Europe stabilized, the number of emigrants decreased. In the 1960s and 1970s, there was an influx of immigrant workers from Mediterranean countries and former Dutch colonies such as Surinam. The late 1990s saw an influx of political refugees from Iraq and Afghanistan.

The Netherlands is experiencing a falling birth rate and an ageing population. In 1900, 44 percent of the population were below the age of 20, and 6 percent were over 64. By the end of the 20th century the figures were 24 percent and 14 percent, respectively.

Opposite: **Children in traditional costumes.**

Below: **Two young women outside the Faculty of Letters at the University of Amsterdam.**

57

WHO ARE THE DUTCH?

The Dutch people are basically a Germanic people, descended from Frisians, Saxons, and Franks. They have been open to external influences for so long that many Dutch are of mixed European ancestry—French Huguenots, Salzburgers, Swiss, Germans, and Portuguese and Eastern European Jews.

During the 20th century the Netherlands' ethnic composition was changed by immigrants from its former colonies—Surinamese from South America and Indonesians from the former Dutch East Indies. Other immigrants have come from Turkey, Morocco, Germany, Britain, and other European countries. In the last few years there have been increasing numbers of immigrants from Afghanistan and Iraq. Today about 9 percent of the Dutch population is of non-Western descent. In 1970 there were fewer than 30 countries represented in the population, but today there are 110.

The greatest population concentration is in the three provinces of North Holland, South Holland, and Utrecht—nearly half of the population lives here. The least densely populated province is Flevoland, which has only one-eighth the population density of South Holland.

THE DUTCH CHARACTER

Perhaps the most notable characteristics of the Dutch are their love of moderation and their respect for law and order. These values are accepted across the whole of society, from the highest to the lowest economic levels. The small size of their country has forced the Dutch to be realistic about liberty and individualism. Having created a country in which so many wish to live, they are highly organized in the way they run their private and national lives. These factors and their trading links with neighboring countries have made them practical people.

Although the native Dutch are quite homogeneous, people from different regions vary in character. In the south, people tend to be more easy-going and relaxed, while in the north, residents are influenced by the more formal reserve of their German neighbors.

At her silver jubilee in 2005, Queen Beatrix made an observation that "some of our matter-of-factness, austerity, and moderation—which were part of the Dutch character—have become less visible." She also urged her people to practice tolerance toward one another.

Opposite: **Couples from different ethnic backgrounds are not uncommon in the Netherlands.**

A SIGN OF WELLNESS?

The Dutch are known to be the tallest people in the world. The national average height for men is 6 feet (182.5 cm) and 5 feet 7 inches (170.5 cm) for women. In comparison the average height in the United States is 5 feet 8 inches (176.7 cm) for men and 5 feet 4 inches (162.8 cm) for women.

Auxologists are people who study human growth. They approach the examination of growth from biological, social, historical, and economic standpoints. Most believe that height is a measure of health and wellness. The height of the Dutch population has been attributed to the high standard of medical care, sensible diet, and healthy lifestyle and environment.

Above: **A Dutch woman in traditional dress from Zeeland Province.**

Opposite: **A boy wearing a traditional costume.**

COSTUMES AND CHARACTERISTICS

Traditional costume is still worn in several towns and villages in the Netherlands. Although some people wear this on a regular basis, others only do so on special days and holidays. In the past the number and variety of regional costumes were much higher than today, but those that remain illustrate the originality that makes Dutch local costume so attractive.

Women's costumes usually consist of a skirt, an apron, and a front-fastening jacket, often with short sleeves. Headdresses, on the other hand, vary widely, including the winged caps of the Volendam women, the silver helmets worn at Staphorst, and the fitted lace caps covering the ears, which are typical of Zeeland Province.

Men's traditional dress usually consists of a black jacket and trousers, enlivened by a brightly colored shirt, rows of silver buttons on the jacket, and a cotton scarf. The finishing touch may be a plain cap, a more eye-catching flat, round, black cap in Zeeland, or a military style cap in Urk.

Marken and Volendam are two villages where traditional costume is still worn on an everyday basis. Both are fishing villages on the western shores of the IJsselmeer. Since the completion of the barrier dam cutting

AN UNDERLYING SENSE OF FUN

Central to the traditional Dutch virtues of hard work and soberness is a warmth and sense of fun. Practical jokes, for instance, are part and parcel of life, and the Dutch are not averse to practicing them on unsuspecting foreigners.

There is a story that during the French occupation of the country, Napoleon Bonaparte ordered that all Dutchmen should be registered by their surnames. At this time, surnames were rarely used—people used their given names and added their fathers' given names. The Dutch were forced to comply with this ruling, but devised ridiculous surnames as a form of protest.

Some of these surnames are still used today—for example, Naaktgeboren, meaning "born naked," Vanhetzelfde, meaning "of the same," Dodeman, or "dead man," and Grizel, or "horror"!

off the Zuiderzee from the North Sea, these villages have come to rely more on tourism than on fishing for their livelihood. The colorful costumes worn in these two villages are a major attraction for visitors.

In most areas more women than men dress in traditional regional costumes. Older people are also more likely to wear traditional costumes on a daily basis, whereas young people usually wear modern clothes.

However, clogs, or *klompen* (KLOM-pehn), are a different matter. Like windmills and tulips, clogs are a universally recognized symbol of the Netherlands. They are still widely used by ordinary Dutch people, both men and women, when engaged in wet and dirty work. When modern dress is exchanged for traditional costume, clogs may be replaced by black leather shoes that often come with silver buckles.

A woman in Marken wearing traditional dress made of colorful chintz.

CHINTZ AND STRIPES

Chintz is a fabric made of cotton and printed in many colors. In the 17th century, the Dutch East India Company imported large amounts of this fabric, which became an important part of traditional dress.

Chintz is a popular fabric even today. At Staphorst, for example, women still wear chintz bodices with large collars decorated with painted flowers above their black- or blue-striped skirts.

Striped patterns are also common elsewhere. In Volendam, traditional fashion calls for a black skirt with a striped apron or a striped skirt with a black apron. A shirt with a flowered design worn under a short-sleeved overblouse, generally black in color and topped with a pointed black bonnet, completes the outfit. On feast days the black bonnet is exchanged for a tall, winged cap.

In Marken, women wear a wide skirt and black apron over a striped petticoat. In summer a red and white striped blouse is worn under a vest with a print in front. The headdress is a lace-and-cotton skullcap.

THE HEROIC AND THE INFAMOUS

Among the heroic and infamous Dutch people of the 20th century are a young girl and a woman—Anne Frank and Mata Hari.

Anne Frank (1929–45), originally from Germany, was a young Jewish girl who came to the Netherlands with her parents in the 1930s. She wrote a diary of her life while hiding from Nazi persecution in Amsterdam during World War II. Her family was eventually betrayed and discovered by the Nazis. Tragically, Anne died in the Bergen-Belsen concentration camp when she was only 15, just a few months before the end of the war. Nonetheless *The Diary of Anne Frank* continues to inspire all who live under the threat of persecution. Today the secret annex in an Amsterdam warehouse (*right*) where her family hid for over two years is one of the city's most popular tourist attractions.

Margaretha Geertruide Zelle (1876–1917) was a courtesan and professional dancer who took the professional name Mata Hari (meaning "the eye of the day"). During World War I she acted as a double agent for both sides, spying for the French and the Germans. In 1917 she was shot by the French for being a German spy.

THE BOY WITH HIS FINGER IN THE DIKE

There is a famous story of a little Dutch boy who saved his village from flooding by putting his finger in a hole in a dike. This stopped the water from getting through and prevented the hole from getting larger, but while waiting for help to come, the little boy died.

Surprisingly this story did not originate in the Netherlands. It was written by a 19th-century American writer, Mary M. Dodge. Although it is fictional, the story reflects some of the characteristics associated with the Dutch. In honor of the fictional little boy's bravery, the Dutch have erected a statue of a boy putting a stone in a dike.

ERASMUS

Desiderius Erasmus, known universally as "The Prince of Humanists," was born in Rotterdam around 1466. The illegitimate son of a priest and his housekeeper, he attended a school run by the Order of the Bretheren of the Common Life—a community devoted to educating and caring for the poor—which had a large intellectual following in Europe.

Erasmus became a monk in 1488 and was ordained a priest in 1492. He studied the classics but found monastic life restrictive and became secretary to the Bishop of Cambrai in 1494. This diplomatic career did not suit him, and he went to the Sorbonne University in Paris to study theology. In Paris, he first met the humanists, whose ideas were to change his life forever.

Erasmus traveled extensively. In England he met Sir Thomas More, author of *Utopia*, who became his best friend. He became a professor for a few years in Louvain, Belgium, and traveled between England, Switzerland, and Italy. He made copies of early Greek New Testament manuscripts that eventually formed the basis of his publication of the Greek New Testament with his own Latin translation.

Erasmus finally settled in Basel, Switzerland, where he published numerous books on classical authors—some Latin and many Greek—including annotated editions of their works. His influence on Reformation philosophers and theologians was enormous. He died in 1536, a great scholar mourned by the civilized world.

"Length of life has no bearing on a man's happiness. It is how well he lived that counts."

—Erasmus

FAMOUS PEOPLE

For such a small country the Netherlands has produced a surprisingly large number of famous people. Many other famous Europeans also migrated to the Netherlands because of war or persecution. They include Carl Linnaeus, the Swedish naturalist, and René Descartes, the French philosopher and mathematician.

Dutch contributions to science have been far-ranging. Christiaan Huygens not only invented the pendulum clock in 1657 but also made major advances in the study of optics. Huygens invented the first successful balance spring for watches and is the originator of the wave theory of light.

Zacharias Janssen made the first microscope, and Antonie van Leeuwenhoek refined it. Leeuwenhoek became the first person to study microbiology by observing bacteria with a microscope. His work was instrumental in disproving the theory of spontaneous generation, which describes living things arising from non-living matter.

In philosophy, religion, and the arts, the Netherlands is represented by several people whose works had a lasting impact on both the country and the European continent.

Thomas-à-Kempis, author of *The Imitation of Christ*, was a 15th-century Augustinian monk who lived near Zwolle in Overijssel. His writings were among the most widely read religious works of his time throughout the whole of Europe.

Hugo Grotius, the famous 17th-century jurist who lived in Delft, was imprisoned for life for his involvement in a religious dispute. Thanks to the resourcefulness of his wife, however, he managed to escape from prison by hiding in a case of books and went to France, where his works on international law were published. He is considered the founder of the science of international law; he was also an accomplished theologian, statesman, and poet.

A statue of Grotius (whose real name was Hugo de Groot).

BARUCH SPINOZA

Son of a Portuguese refugee, Baruch Spinoza was born in Amsterdam in 1632. His family were prosperous merchants and respected members of the Dutch Jewish community.

Spinoza challenged the value of various sacred texts, saying, for example, that there was nothing in the Bible to support the view that God has no body, that angels really exist, or that the soul is immortal. He also advanced the view that the writer of the Pentateuch—the first five books of the Bible—was clearly not well read in physics.

For his views, Spinoza was expelled from Amsterdam and eventually moved to The Hague. He advocated the rational study of the Bible, especially the application of historical methods to biblical sources. He maintained that the inspiration of the Old Testament prophets applied only to moral and theological points, and that their factual beliefs were merely those current at the time. On this basis, he claimed, for example, that many miracles would eventually be rationally explained as scientific knowledge increased over the years.

LIFESTYLE

With 65 percent of the population living in towns, Dutch society is essentially an urban one despite its reputation as an agricultural nation. About five million people—nearly one-third of the total population—are concentrated in the heavily urbanized Randstad area, which encompasses Amsterdam, The Hague, Utrecht, Haarlem, Leiden, and Rotterdam.

Because the Netherlands is so small and densely populated, the Dutch have developed a well-ordered lifestyle in which allowance is made, as far as possible, for citizens to live as they please. This places a great responsibility on each individual to live and let live, and not to inconvenience others.

STANDARDS OF LIVING

Since the end of World War II, the Netherlands has become one of the most successful of the European economies, and the Dutch people have enjoyed a steady increase in their overall standard of living.

Above: **A busy streetside café in a town.**

Opposite: **The Dutch come out in national colors on special occasions, wearing wigs that resemble the Dutch national flag.**

The Dutch standard of living is comparable to that in the United States. The Dutch have 2.5 doctors per 1,000 people, whereas the Americans have 2.6. However the health indicators of the Netherlands often surpass that of the United States. For instance, infant mortality rate is 5.04 for every 1,000 live births in the Netherlands, compared with 6.8 in the United States. American ownership of television sets outstripped the Dutch until recently, but now they are equal, at almost 100 percent ownership.

HOME IS WHERE THE HEART IS

After the devastation of World War II, the Dutch faced a critical housing shortage. They began building apartment blocks but tried to limit the buildings to four or five stories, often with large picture windows overlooking communal gardens. But demand for housing was so great that they were forced to build tower blocks. By 1968, almost half of the buildings under construction had nine stories or more. Despite their best efforts to avoid this situation, many Dutch cities were eventually encircled by huge concrete suburbs.

The greatest dream of the Dutch is to own a house with a garden. Family life at home is all-important, and a lot of time and effort is spent on making homes cozy and welcoming. Since Dutch families spend a great deal of time together, a home atmosphere that is *gezellig* (gheh-ZEL-lig, meaning cozy and inviting) is greatly appreciated.

However, the main obstacle to housing has always been the lack of space. In the 17th century when wealthy merchants built homes alongside

the Amsterdam canals, only houses that were three windows wide were allowed, so houses were made tall, narrow, and deep. Modern townhouses still tend to be tall and narrow, with steep staircases.

Dutch houses have large windows both to let in sunlight and to allow families to see what is going on outside. Many older houses have a spy mirror, called a *sponnetje* (SPO-neh-tcheh), bracketed onto the outside of a window frame to make it easier to look out. The Dutch do not resent people looking into their homes and, until recently, seldom drew their curtains at night.

The Dutch have always been interested in small objects and in detail. Window ledges are likely to have a row of potted plants with a variety of knickknacks—strange shells, paperweights, carvings, and mementos of far-off places. Other household ornaments include prettily framed lace pictures displayed in windows and small paintings inset in front doors.

WOMEN

The Dutch government often makes provisions for women to strengthen their labor opportunities.

Family life is so important to the Dutch that at one time hardly any married women went out to work. As late as 1960, only 3 percent of married women had a full-time job. In the past few decades, the situation has changed radically, particularly since the introduction of equal pay legislation. In 2003, 55 percent of Dutch women were engaged in paid work.

On the domestic front, there have also been many changes since the end of World War II. Until the late 1930s, a wife could not open a bank account without her husband's permission. Both men and women under 30 years of age needed their parents' consent to marry.

Social change has swept away these restrictions, although the law still prohibits one partner in a marriage from selling or renting part of their house, giving excessive gifts to other people, or signing hire-purchase agreements without the other's consent. These measures are all part of a general policy that is designed to keep the family together.

Women's rights organizations have been active in the Netherlands for the past 85 years. Women won the right to vote in 1919. In the 1960s the Dutch feminist movement, called the Dolle Minas gained prominence in calling for greater equality. Literally "Crazy Minas" (Mina is a Dutch female name), six Dutch women in Amsterdam organized a movement to shelter battered women, called Blijf van Mijn Lijf ("blayf vahn mayn

LIBERAL LAWS

The Dutch try to strike a balance between personal freedom and the collective well-being. Amsterdam, for instance, is known the world over for its bawdy night life.

Hard drugs are illegal, but possession of soft drugs is treated more leniently. Marijuana, for instance, has been legal since the 1960s, and anyone may have 1 oz. (28 g) for personal use, although dealing is not allowed. The majority of soft drug users are tolerated, provided their actions do not infringe on the rights of others.

Although euthanasia is technically against the law, the Dutch government allows it to be practiced. It is only allowed to take place under very strict conditions—a terminally ill patient must make a written declaration asking for euthanasia to be performed, and two doctors must be reasonably satisfied that the patient is suffering from unbearable physical and psychological pain and that the disease is incurable.

Policies on these and other controversial issues are often held up as models of enlightened thinking. One such area is that of same-sex marriages. The Netherlands introduced "registered partnerships" in 1998 for same-sex couples, giving them the same rights and duties as those of married couples. Three years later, in 2001, formal civil marriages and adoption for same-sex couples were legalized.

layf," Hands Off My Body) in 1975. In 1983 an amendment to the Dutch constitution prohibited discrimination on the basis of sex. The wage gap between men and women is shrinking. In 1995 Dutch women's hourly wages were 76 percent of men's; but by 2001 the figure was up to 81 percent.

An important figure in the Dutch feminist movement was Aletta Jacobs (1851–1929), who was the first woman doctor in the Netherlands. She opened the world's first birth control clinic in Amsterdam in 1882. When Jacobs tried to vote in 1883, the government responded by specifying that all voters must be male. She was a delegate to the International Congress of Women in 1916, assembled to discuss approaches to ending World War I. The Women's International League for Peace and Freedom, of which she was a founder, grew out of this congress. She campaigned against regulated prostitution and worked for shorter workdays, protective legislation for women workers, sex education, penal reform, women's suffrage, and marriage law reform.

LEARNING THE BASICS

About 70 percent of Dutch children attend private schools. Practically all schools, whether state or private, are coeducational.

Most schools in the Netherlands are run by private, often denominational, organizations, although there are some state schools. Full-time education is compulsory from ages 5 to 16. During this period, education is free, although some schools ask parents to make a financial contribution. Primary schools are for children ages 4 to 12. There are no schools for children under 4, although private play groups and nurseries are popular.

Primary school is designed to prepare children for secondary school. In the first two years children receive lessons in reading, writing, and mathmatics. After this, the syllabus is widened to include Dutch, higher mathematics, writing, history, geography, science, and social studies. In their final year, students also learn English.

Private and state schools are both supported by the state.

LEIDEN UNIVERSITY

The oldest university in the Netherlands is at Leiden, southwest of Amsterdam. It was founded by William of Orange in 1575.

When Leiden was attacked by the Spanish in 1574, the inhabitants opened the sluices and flooded the land. This made it possible for William to send gunboats to raise the siege. As a mark of his gratitude he offered the inhabitants of the city either freedom from taxes or a university. They chose the university.

In the 17th century Leiden University was famous throughout Europe as a center of theology, science, and medicine. This was largely due to Herman Boerhaave, a professor of medicine, botany, and chemistry, who is credited with founding the modern system of medical instruction based on clinical, or "bedside," teaching.

Today Leiden University is one of the most respected universities in the Netherlands.

SECONDARY SCHOOLS

There are three types of secondary schools—general, pre-university, and vocational. Most students at general secondary schools do not go on to a university. After a four- or five-year course of study, they either attend one of the many vocational secondary schools or go directly into industry, trade, or commerce.

Youngsters aiming for a place in university generally go to pre-university secondary schools. These offer a six-year course in preparation for entry into one of the country's eight universities or five *hogescholen* (HO-gheh-SGHO-len), which are equivalent to universities. All Dutch universities are financed directly by the central government, regardless of whether they are state or private organizations.

Adults, including many housewives, are increasingly interested in courses that were not previously available to them. Open Schools and the Open University have been established to cater to adult education.

CARING FOR THE SICK

Compared to many other countries, the Netherlands has excellent health care arrangements. Medical treatment financed by an insurance system is available to all citizens at reasonable prices. For the less well-off, contributions to a state-run health insurance fund are compulsory, with 60 percent of the population covered this way. The better-off are required to take private medical insurance. But in 2006 public and private insurance are set to be integrated. Everyone will be covered by one compulsory standard health insurance program.

Members of a medical insurance program, whether state-run or a private system, enjoy free, or nearly free, medical and hospital treatment. Despite the extensive state involvement in the provision of these facilities, most hospitals are privately run on a denominational basis, although about one-fourth of the hospital beds in the country are in state institutions.

PROVIDING FOR RETIREMENT

Dutch workers also contribute to a state pension program. In some industries, membership in an additional occupational system may be compulsory. The retirement age is 65.

Although there have been proposals to reduce the retirement age to 63 or 62, these plans have been dropped because of the expense involved. Another benefit for retired people, the linking of pension increases to the cost of living so that when the cost of living rises pensioners receive compensatory

Like other groups in the community, the elderly in the Netherlands are represented by non-government groups, such as the Netherlands Platform for the Elderly and Europe (NPOE), which looks into their interests within Europe.

HOFJES—QUIET HOMES FOR THE ELDERLY

The Dutch have always looked after their elderly, poor, and sick. In the 17th century, infirm and elderly relatives were often boarded at *hofjes* (HOF-yehs), institutions that are similar to the British alms houses.

Hofjes were built by wealthy families mainly to create peaceful homes in towns and cities for their aged relatives and employees. Many had well-tended gardens and were entirely surrounded by high walls to keep the street noises at bay. *Hofjes* frequently accommodated several people in self-contained, terraced houses in a quiet street.

Many have survived the passage of time, and a number are still in use today. There are about 50 *hofjes* in Amsterdam alone, some of which have been converted to house students who appreciate the tranquil surroundings.

increments, is also under threat, again because of the cost to the state.

The problems encountered by the Netherlands with regard to healthcare and pensions are not unique. Like many other industrialized nations, the country has an ageing population. Average life expectancy has risen from about 50 years in 1900 to around 76 years for men and 82 years for women at present. As a result there are now fewer people of working age to provide for an increasing number of elderly people.

Other factors also make free medical facilities more expensive: advances in medicine, which widen the range of treatments available, and changes in the major causes of death, such as the increase in cardiovascular diseases and cancer. As a result the Dutch welfare state is under severe financial strain and was especially affected by the world recession in the 1990s. Despite the unpopularity of such moves, many within the government, as well as other sectors of the population, realize that welfare benefits may have to be reduced in order to lighten the financial load.

Commuters travel on Amsterdam's extensive streetcar network.

GETTING AROUND

The Dutch countryside is criss-crossed by numerous rivers and canals. Long before the advent of roads and railways, these waterways provided the country's first passenger transportation system. An extensive railway system was built in the second half of the 19th century. The 20th century brought a comprehensive network of roads and freeways.

Since the land is so flat, there is little to prevent roads from being built totally straight. But, for safety reasons, they are constructed with gentle bends to keep drivers awake. Bridges over the waterways are more common than tunnels. Before World War II there was only one tunnel in the entire country—the Maas Tunnel in Rotterdam—but recently the number of tunnels has increased. One of the recent tunnels to be built is the Westerschelde Tunnel, which joins parts of the Zeeland Province.

Land is in such short supply that the various networks—canal, river, rail, and road—are all woven together to take up the least space possible. In towns, the roads are not laid out in a grid pattern. Narrow bridges over canals and winding streets often make driving difficult in medieval cities that have expanded haphazardly over the years.

In many rural towns and villages, the speed of through traffic is kept to an acceptable level by the old cobbled road surfaces. These have the same function as speed bumps in urban areas. The cobbles cause such alarming vibrations that drivers automatically slow down.

LAND OF THE BICYCLE

In such a small and crowded country, it is not surprising that the official policy is to encourage the use of public transportation, bicycles, and mopeds. These reduce fuel consumption and do less damage to the environment.

In crowded city centers, the bicycle is the ideal mode of transportation when it is not raining. In Utrecht and around Amsterdam's railway station, hundreds of bicycles are parked every day. There are about three times as many bicycles in the Netherlands as cars, and most major roads have bicycle paths alongside. People of all classes ride bicycles—at least one prime minister and some members of the royal family have been known to cycle to work. In towns, cyclists weave deftly in and out of traffic, ringing their bells.

PUBLIC TRANSPORTATION

Public transportation is modern and efficient and carries about one billion passengers a year. A coordinated system of buses, streetcars, and trains links all towns and cities in the country.

Amsterdam and Rotterdam have subway systems, and express trains leave most large towns and cities at frequent intervals. A unified bus and streetcar fare system efficiently divides the country into zones. The same tickets can be used on both urban and regional transportation.

RELIGION

RELIGION HAS ALWAYS BEEN a contentious issue in Dutch society. In fact, there is an old Dutch saying that goes, "One Dutchman, a theologian; two Dutchmen, a church; three Dutchmen, a schism."

Religion was one of the main causes of the Dutch revolt against Catholic Spanish rule in the 16th century. A large proportion of Dutch people have always been solidly Protestant, but a sizeable Catholic minority has always existed. Although publicly proscribed in the past, Catholics were still permitted to worship in private. Nowadays there is no discrimination against adherents of any religion, and in fact such discrimination is illegal.

Generally most Catholics are found in the south, especially in Limburg and North Brabant provinces. Protestants are concentrated in a broad band running from southwest to northeast, from Zeeland to Groningen provinces. Some towns have both Catholic and Protestant areas. Neighboring villages can also have different faiths—Volendam, for example, is a Catholic village, while neighboring Marken is Protestant.

Above: **In 1579 the Reformation led to the conversion of the Utrecht Cathedral from Catholic to Dutch Protestant.**

Opposite: **The interior of a cathedral shows a high, ornate ceiling and a pipe organ that is characteristic of churches throughout Europe.**

ARRIVAL OF CHRISTIANITY

Christianity came to the Netherlands in A.D. 690 when an Anglo-Saxon priest, Willibrord, converted the region to Christianity. He also built the two churches of Saint Salvator and Saint Martin in Utrecht. When these were destroyed by fire, the cathedral in Utrecht was built between 1254 and 1517 on the site of the seventh-century churches. In the Middle Ages, Utrecht was the religious center of the northern provinces.

PROTESTANTS

There are two main reformed churches. The Reformed Church of the Netherlands (Nederlands Hervormde Kerk or NHK) dates back to 1619 and has about three million members. The Reformed Churches in the Netherlands (Gereformeerd Kerken in Nederland or GKN) was founded in 1892 and has about a million members. GKN members are more orthodox and conservative. This group is stronger in rural areas and is traditionally working class. The NHK, on the other hand, has more liberal attitudes on social issues and is more vulnerable to the modern trend toward secularization.

People coming out of a Protestant church.

Membership in these churches has changed significantly in this century. In 1900, 56 percent of the population belonged to either the NHK or the GKN, but in 1990 it was only 28 percent. The figures for the NHK have fallen most dramatically, from 49 percent to just 20 percent over this period. Those who do not belong to any denomination have increased, accounting for 40 percent of the population in 2004, compared to two percent in 1900.

CATHOLICS AND TOLERANCE

During the Middle Ages all of Europe was Catholic, including the Netherlands. But with the spread of the Protestant Reformation in the 16th century, Protestant beliefs and practices, especially those of the reformer John Calvin, became firmly established in the Low Countries.

A Catholic congregation in Amsterdam.

When the Netherlands was part of the Spanish Empire, dissenting Dutch were forced to be Catholics. But after the Dutch regained independence, Calvinism was adopted as the official religion. Even so, the Dutch adopted a tolerant attitude toward other religions, and interference with private worship was rare.

In public the prohibition against Catholicism was upheld. There were no local bishops, so Dutch Catholics were governed by a papal vicar resident in Rome. In private, however, Catholics, Jews, and others were allowed to practice their beliefs. The Dutch authorities also turned a blind eye to the presence of Catholic priests, but they did not tolerate Jesuits because Jesuits vigorously promoted Spanish interests.

The situation changed slowly over time. The Dutch Catholic hierarchy was reestablished in 1853, and by the end of the 19th century, Catholics made up one-third of the population. In the 1960s Catholics outnumbered all the Protestant groups put together.

JANSENISTS AND OLD CATHOLICS

Two substantial Catholic splinter groups—the Jansenists and the Old Catholics—took root in the Netherlands in the 17th and 19th centuries, respectively, and have remained active on Dutch soil.

The Beguinhof in Amsterdam. Many old houses in this courtyard, which dates to the 14th century, housed *begijn* (beh-HAYN), women who chose to live a partial form of convent life.

Jansenism was named after Cornelius Jansen, a Dutch professor of theology at the University of Louvain (in present-day Belgium). Jansenist ideas flourished mostly in France. After a conflict with the Jesuits lasting for 100 years after Jansen's death, the sect was declared heretical by the pope. Its adherents were hunted down in France and many fled to Holland, where they could worship in peace. There are currently about 12,000 Jansenists in the Netherlands, and they claim to have an unbroken line of bishops going back to the time of Saint Peter in Rome.

The Old Catholic Church came into being as a result of the doctrine of papal infallibility promulgated by the Second Vatican Council in 1870. Many of Europe's most learned theologians and bishops did not accept this doctrine, which they said was unknown to the Church for the previous 1,800 years. They split from Rome and set up their own church—Catholic in every way except in the matter of the infallibility of the pope—and became known as the Old Catholics.

OTHER RELIGIONS

The next largest group in the Netherlands, after the vast majority of Christians, is the Muslims, who make up 6 percent of the population. These are mainly accounted for by the immigrant population of Moroccans, Turks, Iraqis, Afghans, and Iranians. Hindus, Jews, and Buddhists make up just 3 percent of the population. The Jewish community is mainly concentrated in Amsterdam.

PROTESTANTISM AND CALVINISM

In 1517 Martin Luther nailed his 95 "theses" to the door of Wittenburg Church in Germany. This started the Protestant Reformation, which changed the face of religious practices in Europe.

Luther's protests focused on doctrinal issues and on corruption within the Catholic Church. Protestantism spread quickly to the Low Countries. By about 1530 the Anabaptists—a breakaway Protestant sect—were more numerous than the Lutherans. The Anabaptists rejected the baptism of infants in favor of adult baptism and had revolutionary views on other matters. They caused an uproar by refusing to swear allegiance to the prince or to serve in the armed forces.

With the passing of time, Calvinism, a form of Protestantism advocated by John Calvin, became the dominant Protestant sect in the Netherlands. Calvin believed that the church should have control of its own affairs and authority over its own members. He also expressed the view that a formal church was unnecessary for man's salvation—he believed that God speaks directly to man, not through the structures of the church, and freely bestows divine grace where he wishes. This does not mean, however, that the state is unnecessary. On the contrary, without it there would be anarchy.

Calvinism originated in France and spread largely because of the practice of public preaching and open-air services. By 1560 it was firmly established in the Low Countries. It appealed strongly to both the working classes and the middle classes because of its glorification of work and its emphasis on discipline. After the War of Independence with Spain, Calvinist zeal became stronger, and other religions, especially Catholicism, were forced underground.

Statue of Erasmus, the famous Dutch religious scholar who translated the New Testament from Greek into Latin.

THE PILLARIZATION OF SOCIETY

"Pillarization" or *verzuilen* (ver-ZUEH-len) is an important factor in the structure of Dutch society.

The Dutch hold two principles very dear: first, the validity of their personal opinions, and second, the belief that different views should be given due respect. For this reason, a type of society founded on a number of "pillars" has developed, each representing different groups within the population. Each group is distinguished by a set of beliefs, and its members are organized independently of members of other pillars.

These pillars are, in a sense, the foundations of Dutch society and they influence many areas of life in the Netherlands. Each pillar has its own newspapers, schools, trade unions, hospitals, football clubs, and even universities—the Protestant Free University of Amsterdam and the Radboud University of Nijmegen are two prime examples. When broadcasting started in the 1920s, there were radio stations run by the Protestant, Catholic, Socialist, and other pillars. Even today the Dutch watch television channels that are still sponsored by the same organizations.

At present there are three main pillars—Protestant, Catholic, and a third pillar that encompasses a number of neutral groups. Others may focus on a specific political viewpoint. However, now that the population is relatively secular, pillarization is less widespread.

POST-WAR CHANGE

The privations of World War II and the pressures of modern society have considerably altered the Dutch outlook on life. Perhaps the biggest change has resulted from the decline in the number of churchgoers and the increase in the number of agnostics.

Dutch Catholics are the most liberal in Europe. In modern times, pop music and evangelical methods have been adopted to attract young people to Catholic services. Some Dutch priests have even given up celibacy—a topic hotly debated in the Catholic Church today.

In the past the pillars helped maintain a stable, though perhaps inward-looking society. In the last 40 years, however, the pillarization system has declined with loosening religious ties.

In the 1990s the divisions within society represented by the pillars were seen as much less important, especially in the eyes of the younger generation. Intermarriage between people of different faiths is common, and even the religion-based political parties have started to merge. The Protestant and Catholic parties united in the 1960s to form the Christian Democratic Appeal, which now dominates the political center ground. In the cities and to some extent in the countryside, the division of society into rigid sectors has almost disappeared.

10.-

10.-

VASTE PLANT
AKELEI
1 voor 3,-
2 voor 5,-

GAZANIA
1 voor 2,-
3 voor 5,-

't touch
toccare
as toucher
t anfassen
aankomen

Don't touch
Non toccare
Ne pas toucher
Nicht anfassen

LANGUAGE

THE DUTCH LANGUAGE IS spoken all over the Netherlands, in addition to northern Belgium, where it is known as Flemish. It is also used along with native languages in the Netherlands Antilles in the Caribbean. Afrikaans, a language spoken widely by the white population in South Africa, is derived from the Dutch language. However, Afrikaans has been separated from Dutch for so long that it has developed a markedly different pronunciation and grammar.

Dutch is basically a Germanic language, and is considered the simplest of Western European languages after English, in terms of grammar. It has a large number of imported words, that come mainly from English and French. However, considering how long the Netherlands was dominated by Spain, there are remarkably few Spanish words in the language.

Many Dutch words are similar to English words, although the spelling may be different. For example, *koek* (cook) means cook, *noord* (nord) means north, and *straat* (straaht) means street. *Melk* (melk) means milk, and *oud* (out) and *niewe* (neew) mean old and new, respectively.

INFLUENCE ON ENGLISH

Dutch expertise in sailing and navigation has also led to many Dutch nautical terms finding their way into the English language, such as "smuggler" and "reef." The Dutch also contributed words to American English—these include "boss," "waffle," "cookie," "duffle," "snoop," and "spook." Dutch immigrants in the Cape Province in South Africa contributed "commando" and "trek."

Dutch influence can also be seen in American place names—Harlem and Brooklyn in New York City are named after the towns of Haarlem in North Holland and Breukelen in Utrecht. In fact New York City was formerly called Nieuw Amsterdam by its early Dutch settlers.

The word "Dutch" comes from Duitch, *which was originally used to distinguish the language of ordinary people from Church Latin. In due course, "Dutch" was also used to describe the people and led to the modern German word* Deutch *(as in Deutchland, meaning Germany). In the 15th and 16th centuries, the English used the word "Dutch" to mean German, but it was gradually restricted to the Netherlanders and their language.*

Opposite: **A flower seller uses several languages in his signs.**

87

Newspapers and sign-boards showing the different languages spoken in the country.

PRONUNCIATION

Although a simplified, phonetic spelling was introduced after World War II, Dutch pronunciation can still be confusing. Written Dutch looks difficult until one becomes familiar with the spelling conventions.

For example, the combination *ij* is considered a single letter in Dutch and is pronounced "eye." Words beginning with *ij* capitalize both letters, as in IJsselmeer. In the phone directory, *ij* is listed after the letter *y*.

The letters *ui*, as in *huis*, are pronounced like *ou* in "house." The letter *g* is pronounced *kh*, a guttural sound rather like the Scottish word *loch*. The name of the famous Dutch painter Van Gogh is pronounced "van go" in the United States, "van goff" in Great Britain, and "van khoch" in Dutch. The letters *jk* are pronounced without the *j* sound but with a *y* sound—for example, the word *dijk* is pronounced "dayk."

DIALECTS AND OTHER LANGUAGES

The Netherlands has a large number of dialects, generally named after the regions in which they are spoken. The regions of Veluwe, Groningen, Drenthe, and Gelderland all have their own dialects. Frankish is spoken on the German border, and dialects of Vlaams (or Flemish) are found in the south in Brabant and

Limburg. Frisian, spoken in Friesland Province, is classified as a distinct language. It is not understood by ordinary Dutch-speaking people.

Standard Dutch is known as *Algemeen Beschaafd Nederlands* (AHL-heh-main Behs-SHAAHFT NAY-der-lands), meaning General Cultural Dutch. It is taught in schools and used for official purposes.

Since the Netherlands is surrounded by larger European countries, most Dutch people learn a second language. English is the most popular, followed by German and French. There is a remarkably high standard of spoken English, especially in the towns and cities. Nowadays the use of English words in Dutch is much greater than any other language. Many French words entered the language during the reign of Napoleon. Still prevalent today is the use of the French expression for "please," *s'il vous plait*, either spelled out or abbreviated as *svp* on public signs.

FRISIAN

Frisian is a language of Celtic origin used in Friesland, the province to the north of the IJsselmeer. It is similar to early English in many respects and, in fact, it is the closest living foreign language to English. It contains many words familiar in English, such as the words "bread" and "butter," instead of the Dutch *brood* (brood) and *boter* (BOH-ter).

The Frisian language is spoken by about half the province's population of 600,000 and is taught in schools as the second language. Many Frisians speak Frisian at home and Dutch at work. In the streets a sort of "town Frisian" is used that combines Dutch and Frisian, speakers choosing words from each language to suit their immediate needs. Signposts in Friesland are frequently in both Frisian and Dutch.

Outside of the Netherlands, Frisian speakers are only found in certain parts of Germany.

The harsh, guttural sch *sound is a particularly difficult combination of consonants. Apart from the Dutch, only the Scots can pronounce it correctly. During World War I, the name of a seaside resort, Scheveningen (SGHAY-veh-ning-en), was used to test whether speakers were Dutch or German. If they pronounced the* sch *in the typical soft German fashion, they were suspected of being German spies.*

AS THE DUTCH SAY …

The Dutch have a variety of proverbs and sayings. Some are the same as in English, such as "Many hands make light work," "All cats are black in the dark," and "No smoke without fire." Some have close English equivalents, such as:

Dutch: "Don't disturb a broody hen."
English: "Let sleeping dogs lie."

Dutch: "Carrying water to the sea."
English: "Carrying coals to Newcastle."

Dutch: "He doesn't show the back of his tongue."
English: "He plays his cards close to his chest."

A few sayings have English equivalents, but the Dutch version has its origins in situations or events known only to the Dutch. While in English we say, "The die is cast," the Dutch say somewhat mysteriously, "The bullet is through the church." Similarly, the Dutch form of "Much ado about nothing" is "Much shouting but little wool."

Some Dutch sayings do not have any obvious English equivalents. These include: "If one sheep is over the dam, more will follow" and "When the fox is preaching, farmer guard your chickens."

RADIO AND TELEVISION

Radio broadcasting started in the Netherlands in 1928. Unlike radio stations elsewhere in Europe, programming is left to private enterprise, with little or no government interference. There are five national radio stations broadcasting on AM or FM. Radio 3 is a pop station, and Radio 4 transmits only classical music. The others feature varied content.

Radio Nederland, an independent station, is the Dutch equivalent of the Voice of America. It transmits programs in Dutch, English, Spanish, Portuguese, Indonesian, Arabic, French, Sranan Tongo (for Surinam), and Papiamento (for the Netherlands Antilles).

Television broadcasting dates from 1951, and there are currently three national channels. Dutch viewers are also able to watch programs from several surrounding countries, especially neighboring England, Germany, and Belgium. Most households are connected to the cable network, and satellite television is also gaining in popularity.

Advertising generates income for both radio and television stations. The commercials are subject to a government code to ensure they are in good taste and conform to legal requirements. Some advertising is restricted. Alcoholic drinks, for example, may only be advertised in limited circumstances, and tobacco advertising is totally prohibited.

FREEDOM OF SPEECH

Freedom of speech is one of the cornerstones of Dutch democracy, and for this reason the government encourages the expression of a wide range of opinions in the press and broadcasting organizations.

Newspapers enjoy various tax and postal concessions, and broadcasting organizations receive financial aid from the sale of licenses. A Press Fund was set up in 1974 to assist newspapers and news weeklies to receive financial support from the government.

Nearly all newspapers are sold by subscription and are delivered directly to people's homes. Just a few are sold in roadside stands and supermarkets. Most national papers are morning papers. There are about 4,000 periodicals covering all aspects of life and leisure, including radio and television guides, popular magazines, scientific and trade journals, and news weeklies.

A poster in Dutch advertising candy.

The Dutch prefer casual greetings to more formal forms of address.

FORMS OF ADDRESS

The Dutch are generally informal in their dealings with one another, both in speech and in writing. Although an aristocracy still exists, it has integrated well with the rest of the population. Thus, in Great Britain, for example, one would use a title such as "Sir" or "Lord" when addressing a titled person, but in the Netherlands this is not usually so, except on the most formal of occasions.

When writing to a Dutch person, the address on the envelope includes the Dutch equivalent of "Mr." or "Mrs." "Mr." is written as *Hr*, standing for *Heer*—short for *Mijnheer* (mehn-NEER). For "Mrs.," the Dutch write *Mw* or *Mevr*, standing for *Mevrouw* (mehv-FRAOW). "Miss" is *Mejuffrouw* (may-YOU-fraow) and is abbreviated to *Mej*. Thus, a letter to a Mr. and Mrs. Jansen would be addressed to *Hr & Mw Jansen*. A letter to Hr Jansen's daughter, Marieke, would be addressed to *Mej M. Jansen*.

If the precise details of a person's titles and qualifications are not known to the writer, the letters "SSTT" are sometimes added after the name of the adressee. These stand for *Salvis Titulis*, a Latin term, and indicate that the sender does not know what title or form of address to use but means no disrespect by omitting the title.

When meeting other people for the first time, the Dutch address them as *Mijnheer* or *Mevrouw*, just as we might say, "Hello, Mr. Smith." Generally, however, the Dutch prefer to be informal and quickly move on to using first names.

LEARNING A LITTLE DUTCH

To greet someone, the Dutch say "hallo," similar to the English "hello." Depending on the time of day, one would then say, "*Goede morgen*" (HOO-deh MOR-hen, good morning), or "*Goede middag*" (HOO-deh MEE-dagh, good afternoon), or "*Goede avond*" (HOO-deh AH-vunt, good evening). A visitor might also hear "*Goeie morgen*" (HOO-yeh MOR-hen), "*Goeie middag*," or "*Goeie avond*," which are more colloquial ways of saying these greetings. "*Aangenaam*" (AHN-heh-nam) means "pleased to meet you."

To say goodbye, one could say, "*Tot volgende keer*" (toht vohl-hen-deh-KAYR, see you next time). "*Dag*" (dach) also means goodbye, and "*Tot ziens*" (toht-SEENS) means "See you."

ARTS

FOR SUCH A SMALL COUNTRY, the Netherlands has had a surprisingly large impact on the world of art. Old masters such as Rembrandt and Vermeer have long enjoyed international fame, as have Van Gogh and Mondriaan. Meanwhile, on a more popular level, M.C. Escher has achieved a cult following for his intriguing drawings and engravings, which combine science and art.

The Dutch place great importance on bringing art and culture into the community at large. Painting and sculpture are used extensively to enhance the environment. Housing estates are planned with sculptures in mind, and artists are commissioned to provide eye-catching pieces. In the development of the new town of Zoetermeer near The Hague, teams of architects, planners, sociologists, artists, and sculptors worked together to make art an integral part of daily life rather than just an accessory.

Opposite: **Visitors admire a painting in the Amsterdam History Museum.**

Below: **A craftsman makes clogs in his workshop.**

SUPPORT FOR THE ARTS

The government actively supports art and artists by subsidizing literary and artistic magazines, theater workshops, and other experimental projects. Municipal councils often commission artists to produce works for public buildings. Similarly, ballet, modern dance, and music receive substantial official sponsorship.

These policies have contributed to a resurgence of artistic activity in the past few years. Amsterdam is now one of the leading artistic centers in Europe, with thousands of painters, sculptors, musicians, and writers coming together to create an atmosphere similar to that of Paris in the 1930s.

The most famous and important art museum in the country is the Rijksmuseum in Amsterdam. It contains a superb collection of art treasures by Flemish, Dutch, Italian, Spanish, and French masters from the 15th to the 19th centuries.

MASTERS OF THE GOLDEN AGE

The artistic reputation of the Dutch is primarily built on the genius of the great masters of the 17th century—Rembrandt van Rijn, Frans Hals, Jan Vermeer, and Jan Steen—but in addition to these, the Netherlands has produced a host of great painters.

The arts of the Golden Age were primarily intended to decorate the homes and celebrate the achievements of rich merchants. As a result, the subjects painted were mainly secular and provided later generations with a remarkable record of the daily life of the times. Dutch artists excelled in detailed portraits of daily life, domestic interiors, guild portraits, and landscapes to decorate the houses of the wealthy.

Jan Vermeer painted quiet interior scenes with painstaking precision. Despite the simplicity of his subject matter, his use of light, vivid tones, geometry, and composition raised his portrayal of domestic scenes to the level of masterpieces. Paintings such as *The Kitchen Maid*, *The Young Woman Reading a Letter*, and *Girl with a Pearl Earring* are examples of his choice of subjects and skill.

Jan Steen is noted for his cheerful pictures, often of inn scenes, executed with verve and delicacy and painted very much from life. Steen was an innkeeper because he could not make a living from painting. In contrast, Jacob van Ruisdael created dark, romantic landscapes with somber clouds, gnarled forests, and ruined castles.

Group portraits of guild members, civic guards, surgeons, almshouse regents, and other dignitaries are also characteristic of this period. These were the specialty of two outstanding figures—Frans Hals and Rembrandt van Rijn. Frans Hals is remembered for magnificent canvases such as *The Banquet of the Officers of the St. George Militia of Haarlem*, as well as for smaller portraits like that of *The Jolly Toper*.

Whether he was painting individuals or groups, Rembrandt—undoubtedly one of the world's greatest artists—emphasized the human element in his portraits. In later life, he developed a taste for strong contrasts between light and shade, and painted such dramatic scenes as *The Night Watch* and *The Anatomy Lesson of Dr. Tulp*. He is also famous for his self-portraits, which show him in his youth, at the height of his career as a successful master, and later moving into a sad old age.

The Night Watch, one of Rembrandt's most famous paintings, hangs in the Rijksmuseum.

Most of the Netherlands' artistic treasures from this age are contained in the Rijksmuseum in Amsterdam, the Mauritshuis in The Hague, and the Frans Hals Museum in Haarlem.

Artists from before the Golden Age include Jan van Eyck, who founded the Flemish school in the 15th century, Hieronymus Bosch, known for his fantastic religious paintings, and Pieter Brueghel, who excelled in everyday scenes.

VAN GOGH AND MODERN ARTISTS

Vincent Van Gogh was born near Breda, North Brabant in 1853. His first pictures were painted in somber colors, but after moving to Paris in 1886 and coming into contact with the Impressionists, his pictures became more luminous and colorful.

A couple of years later, he went to Arles in southern France to shut himself away from the world and to paint undisturbed. But he was desperately lonely and under great strain, mainly because he was trying to make a living from painting to repay his brother who was supporting him. He painted frenzied wheat fields and tormented olive and cypress trees twisted by the *mistral* (mis-TRAAHL), a wind that blows across southern France. From time to time, he lapsed into temporary insanity and had to be hospitalized, but continued painting during lucid intervals. Tragically, in 1890, he took his own life.

Van Gogh used color and form to convey what he felt about the scene before his eyes. He distorted shapes and used color in unusual ways. He frequently applied paint in broad brush strokes, laying on the color thickly.

During his lifetime, Van Gogh only managed to sell one painting, but over a hundred years after his death, his painting *The Sunflowers* was sold for $53 million.

Willem de Kooning, a Dutchman who emigrated to the United States, was famous for his abstract expressionist paintings. Other modern painters and sculptors include Wessel Couzijn, Carel Visser, Jan Dibbets, Ad Dekkers, Ger van Elk, and Martha Röling.

An artist with popular appeal, M.C. Escher, has achieved a cult following for his almost surreal patterns of fish and birds and his intriguing optical illusions.

PIET MONDRIAAN

The abstract painter Piet Mondriaan was born in Amersfoort in 1872. While earning a degree in education at the insistence of his family, he experimented with painting, starting with still lifes and landscapes, often in subdued colors and on subjects chosen from his surroundings in Amsterdam.

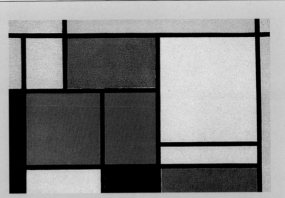

Mondriaan moved to Paris in early 1912 after seeing some early cubist works by Pablo Picasso and Georges Braque. There he embarked on his own cubist period, which lasted until 1917. From 1913 onward his style became increasingly abstract but kept to the general cubist conventions of a limited range of colors and focusing interest toward the center of the picture.

In further reducing the elements in his compositions, Mondriaan began to avoid curved lines and diagonal accents, and concentrated on using only vertical and horizontal lines. From this point he began eliminating all pictorial matter from his paintings, leaving only the simplest of forms.

Mondriaan became the leading figure of a group of artists who called their artistic movement *de Stijl*, or the Style. Their aims were the rejection of realism and the restriction of a picture to what they considered its most basic elements of composition and color—straight lines and right angles, and the three primary colors of yellow, red, and blue along with black, white, and gray.

In 1940 Mondriaan emigrated to New York City, where he continued to develop this abstract style. His paintings represent a personal striving for beauty through extreme purity of line and simple harmony.

THEATER AND CINEMA

The Dutch are not enthusiastic theatergoers, and theater is subsidized to ensure its survival. Most plays performed are translations of English, French, or German works. Similarly most movies shown are from the United States, France, Great Britain, and Germany, with Dutch subtitles.

Both forms of entertainment suffer from a language problem—a Dutch movie or play may meet with great success at home, but it is unlikely to be noticed elsewhere because Dutch is not spoken internationally. Similarly, in Dutch literature, there are many excellent writers, but their work seldom reaches an international audience. However, some younger writers are trying to overcome the language problem by writing in English.

Modern Dutch writers include Simon Vestdijk, whose works have been translated into many languages. However, his international success has not matched his great talent.

MUSIC AND DANCE

A street musician plays an entertaining tune on his accordion.

Music plays a central part in Dutch life. There are few families in which no one plays an instrument or sings in a choir. In the country as a whole, just about every town has its own amateur orchestra, chamber music ensemble, or choral society. The big cities have their own symphony orchestras, and Amsterdam's Royal Concertgebouw Orchestra has achieved worldwide fame under the baton of Bernard Haitink. Opera still plays only a small role on the cultural scene.

Dutch composers are not well known internationally. The most famous is perhaps Jan Pieterzoon Sweelinck (1562–1621), who was an organist in Amsterdam. Modern composers who are recognized outside the country are William Pijper and Henk Badings.

Unlike music, which has deep roots in Dutch society, ballet has been an established part of the Dutch cultural life for a comparatively short time. On the other hand, since World War II, modern dance forms have become extremely popular with performers and audiences alike. Dance festivals are held annually to showcase latest dance trends.

BARREL ORGANS AND CARILLONS

Such is their love of music that the Dutch contrive to have it everywhere, not just in the concert hall. On a fine day, the streets and parks are alive with its sound. Street music comes from two contrasting sources—gaudily decorated barrel organs in ordinary shopping streets and melodious carillons in municipal and ecclesiastical buildings.

With their cheerful toe-tapping music and moving figures, the barrel organs entertain shoppers and passers-by. They are so popular that some towns retain their own barrel organs for regular use.

In contrast with the honky-tonk music of the barrel organ, the carillon with its fixed bells—sometimes as many as 50—produces a gentler kind of music. The bells were originally activated by a clockwork mechanism, but modern carillons are generally played by a *carilloneur* (cah-ree-yon-NEUR) sitting at a keyboard.

Carillon music enjoys such a following that there has been a school for carilloneurs at Amersfoort since 1953, and there is a carillon museum at Asten, near Eindhoven.

The Netherlands is famous for its pottery. A product of the Golden Age, blue-and-white pottery called Delftware is still made in Delft, continuing an artistic tradition of over 300 years.

STYLISH URBAN ARCHITECTURE

Above: **Dutch gabled houses. Gables come in many different forms—some are stepped, others bell-shaped or triangular; some are plain, and others have decorations cut into the stone facings.**

Below: **The famous cube houses in Rotterdam are examples of unique, modern, Dutch architectural designs.**

Dutch urban architecture has been famous for centuries, and in the post-war period architects have gained a wide reputation for innovation. In recent years Dutch town planners have developed a number of interesting solutions to the problem of housing an expanding population.

The wealthy merchant classes of the Golden Age built impressive homes, but the limited space restricted both size and design. In Amsterdam, when the city's original concentric canals were under construction, the city fathers restricted the width of the canalside houses to the width of three windows. As a result people had to build their mansions tall and deep.

At first glance these solid buildings appear to be identical, but a closer look reveals a wealth of detail and variety. Buildings were constructed using small bricks and faced with stone—an expensive commodity because of its scarcity in the country. The houses' most eye-catching features are the traditional Dutch gables.

DUTCH FURNITURE

With the home playing such an important part in daily life, the Dutch have a taste for fine and solid furniture. In terms of design, their furniture reached its artistic peak at the end of the 16th century.

Recreation of a room in an upper-class home of the 19th century, with furniture of the period.

Dutch Renaissance wardrobes are among the most famous items of the period. They had four doors, were topped with a cornice sometimes carved with plants, and sat on a wide plinth. Decorative touches included intricate carvings, featuring lions, caryatids, scrolls, and various geometrical designs. Regional variations include the Zeeland wardrobe, which was wider than it was high, while Frisian wardrobes had only two doors.

In the 17th and 18th centuries there was a flowering of marquetry and inlay work. Ebony, tortoise-shell, ivory, and metals were inlaid into desks, writing tables, cabinets, and drawers.

Today Dutch furniture design is unique in its innovative approach to style and function, taking into consideration smaller spaces of modern homes. Furniture such as armchairs and work desks combine practical use and comfort with an understated contemporary elegance.

LEISURE

THE IMPORTANCE OF FAMILY LIFE ensures that leisure pursuits in the Netherlands are family- and home-oriented.

In the mid 1950s a nationwide survey found that the Dutch spent most of their spare time at home. Another survey in the 1970s found that although changes in working practices and lifestyle had increased the number of leisure hours, the Dutch still spent a lot of time at home. In the 1990s although there is increased participation in sporting activities, led by an interest in soccer, the Dutch are still a home-loving people.

There are plenty of opportunities for organized, active recreation, such as sports. Even so, only about a quarter of all leisure time is given over to sports and much less to public entertainment, such as visiting the theater or going out to dinner.

Left: **The Keukenhof Gardens are a good spot for a leisurely stroll.**

Opposite: **Locals and tourists visit a fair.**

REST AND RELAX

Traditionally the Dutch tend not to indulge in entertainment outside the home. Long, cold, winter evenings make a cozy home seem especially inviting. There is little incentive to venture out, and a comfortable evening

Dinner and entertainment on a barge.

at home with the newspaper, a good book, or an entertaining program on television seems inviting.

After getting home from work, people sometimes relax with wine, beer, or a *borrel* (BOR-rohl)—a small glass of Dutch gin, drunk chilled and undiluted, but not on ice. After the evening meal the family settles down to enjoy time together.

Younger people are likely to be out and about during the evenings, visiting friends, dancing at a disco, and enjoying themselves in a lively fashion. For their parents, the chances are that catching up on the news is the first priority. Some Dutch newspapers are evening editions, so those staying in may spend a part of the evening going through the news. Holland has one of the highest newspaper subscriptions per capita in the world.

The Dutch are great readers in other ways also. Public libraries lend millions of books per year. So many people are multilingual that bookshops carry large stocks of English, French, and German books. Foreign bestsellers are likely to be translated into Dutch and published in paperback editions.

Television is another great draw, and most households have their own set. There are plenty of channels to choose from. Many television programs are broadcast

Playing board games is a popular after-dinner family pastime in many Dutch homes.

from Great Britain, the United States, and Germany, and there is easy access to programs from neighboring European countries. However good the entertainment, many families still spend the evening just chatting, listening to music, or making music together. Friends may also drop in for a chat over a cup of tea or coffee or perhaps some cake.

Weekend activities might include a shopping expedition on Saturday and a leisure excursion on Sunday. Because going to church is no longer very common, families have outings together—a walk or a visit to a local event or a nearby museum. Weekends are also a good time to meet up with friends and relatives and have a relaxing day.

Sports are gradually playing a more important part in Dutch life compared to a century ago, when only 0.6 percent of the population took part in sports. Today there are facilities for around 60 different sports. Nearly half the population older than 15 participate in sports every week. There are also several local and international exhibitions that are held frequently, such as the Amsterdam Boat Show and the Bicycle Show, where people can find out more about the latest models for their favorite recreation.

NATIONAL SPORTS

The Dutch have long been passionate about soccer, which they call *voetbal* (VOOT-bahl). The Royal Netherlands Football Association has almost 1 million members. In the 1970s the Dutch star soccer player, Johan Cruyff, was among the most famous and talented players in the world. A number of Dutch teams rank among the best in the world—Ajax Amsterdam, Feyenoord Rotterdam, and PSV in Eindhoven have a tremendous national as well as local following. Tennis, with 500,000 players belonging to various clubs, is the second largest organized sport in the country.

The Dutch have been walking and cycling—all activities with their roots deep in the Dutch landscape and history—far longer than they have been playing soccer and tennis.

In summer, the Dutch countryside offers many opportunities for swimming, sailing, and water-skiing in specially created watersports areas, often in newly reclaimed parts of the land or on the shores of the Netherlands' numerous lakes. Towns and cities have indoor and outdoor pools, and the 150-mile (240-km) coastline along the North Sea caters to those who seek open spaces.

Once the sport of the privileged, boating and sailing is brought within the reach of most of the population through clubs and sailing schools. Visiting boat shows also fuel the interests of boating enthusiasts.

SKATING

The Dutch are great skating devotees, and nearly all Dutch children learn to skate. During an exceptionally cold winter—about once every five or six years—the canals freeze over, and adults and children collect their skates and take to the ice. Fortified by hot chocolate sold on wayside stalls, they skate on the frozen canals across the polders and around the towns. However, frozen canals are now becoming more rare, thought to be due to global warming caused by the increase in "greenhouse gases," such as carbon dioxide, in the atmosphere.

When canal skating is not possible, skating enthusiasts have to make do with the many artificial ice rinks that have been built in recent years, which are also used for speed skating, figure skating, and ice hockey.

LOCAL SPORTS

Several quaint local sports have survived to the present day. The most widely known is *fierljeppen* (feerl-YEP-pen), or vaulting over canals or wide ditches with the help of a long pole. It is a Friesland specialty and at one time was the farmers' only means of crossing ditches and waterlogged land.

The *Ringrijden* (RING-ray-den) is held at Middelburg in Zeeland Province each August. Riders on horseback aim a lance at small, suspended rings. The winner of this competition receives a trophy from the queen.

Opposite: **Skating on frozen canals in winter and sailing in summer are popular activities that take place at many lakes and along the long coast of the Netherlands.**

Below: **A participant in the *Ringrijden* takes aim with his lance.**

VACATIONS ABROAD

The Dutch enjoy the warmth and sunshine of the Mediterranean countries, so many of them head for Spain or Italy for their vacations. With rising incomes, more Dutch people can now afford to vacation abroad. Inexpensive package tours have made dreams of sunshine-filled days come true.

Germany, France, Belgium, Luxembourg, and Great Britain also receive their share of Dutch visitors. The number of vacationers who drive their cars abroad on road trips has also increased, especially when going to a neighboring country.

The seaside resort town of Scheveningen near The Hague attracts many visitors in summer.

Picnics and beach sports at Grevelingendam in Zeeland Province. With the construction of dams in this delta region, Zeeland's beaches have become a popular recreation area.

VACATIONS AT HOME

For every Dutch family that vacations abroad, there are just as many who stay at home. Many go for camping holidays where they can sail or swim, relax on the beach, and take life easy.

Cycling tours are common, and it is common to meet a family pedaling through the woods or over coastal dunes. The land is criss-crossed by bicycle paths. Many pass through pretty countryside and make cycling a pleasure. But the sun does not always shine, and cyclists frequently have to struggle against strong winds and rain blowing across the polders.

Like cycling, walking is also well organized and is served by several clubs. Real enthusiasts, of which there are many thousands, young and old, may take part in the annual four-day walking event in Nijmegen. This takes place in July and involves hikes of up to 30 miles (48 km).

Another walking possibility is *wadlopen* (WAHD-loh-pen), or mudwalking on the mud flats from the mainland across the Waddenzee to the West Frisian islands. This popular walk is possible only at low tide.

FESTIVALS

THE DUTCH CELEBRATE a variety of festivals and holidays. Some are religious festivals, some commemorate historic events, and some reflect various aspects of Dutch culture and lifestyle.

THE QUEEN'S BIRTHDAY

The Queen's Official Birthday—*Koninginnedag* (koh-nee-HEE-neñ-dagh)—on April 30 is a public holiday. It has not always been a public holiday, and it has not always been celebrated on the same date. Queen Wilhelmina celebrated her first birthday as queen in 1891 on her real birthday—August 31. Since this day also fell at the end of the school summer vacations, it soon became a holiday for all Dutch schoolchildren.

Wilhelmina was succeeded by Juliana in 1948, and Koninginnedag was moved to the new queen's real birthday—April 30. In the meantime, the floral tributes that had been offered initially to her grandmother, Queen Emma, on her birthday on August 2, had grown first into a grand parade and then into a national celebration on Queen Juliana's birthday. It also became the tradition for everyone to be given a day off work.

In 1980 when Queen Beatrix succeeded to the throne on April 30, it was decided that this day—also her mother's birthday—be retained as the monarch's official birthday and a public holiday for all citizens. One reason was because the weather on January 31, Queen Beatrix's actual birthday, is often unsuitable for outdoor celebrations.

Opposite: **A participant in the Groningen parade.**

PUBLIC HOLIDAYS

January 1	New Year's Day
March/April	Good Friday
March/April	Easter Monday
April 30	The Queen's Official Birthday
May 5	Liberation Day
variable	Ascension Day
variable	Whit Monday
December 25	Christmas
December 26	Boxing Day

REMEMBRANCE AND LIBERATION

Remembrance Day on May 4 commemorates those who died during World War II. Although this is not a public holiday, the whole country observes a two-minute moment of silence at 8 P.M.—trains, trams, and all road traffic comes to a stop, and the whole country is at a standstill.

These graves commemorate World War II resistance fighters.

Just before 8 P.M., Queen Beatrix lays a wreath at the War Memorial in the Dam in front of the Royal Palace in Amsterdam. The prime minister and senior members of the government are also present.

Liberation Day on May 5 commemorates the end of the German occupation period in 1945. It is a national holiday only every five years. However, civil servants have Liberation Day as a holiday every year.

CARNIVAL IN THE SOUTH

February is carnival time, especially in southern provinces, such as Limburg, which are largely Catholic. The seven weeks leading up to the start of Lent constitute the carnival season.

The tradition goes back to the 15th century, when the south was ruled by the Dukes of Burgundy, and the people of the region acquired a taste for open-air theaters, banquets, and riotous celebrations. Major carnivals are held seven weeks before Easter. Some draw participants

and spectators from far and wide; some are almost private affairs of interest only to residents of the town staging the event. Preparations for carnivals start many weeks in advance, and there is a great feeling of community spirit. Bands practice, songs are composed, processional floats are designed, shops are decorated, and gatherings enliven the cold winter days and nights.

On Carnival Day itself, the town resounds with music—in the street, in restaurants, and in the procession. Thousands of visitors throng the sidewalks to see the fun, which often verges on the outrageous. Music, dance, and colorful parades are a feature of Carnival Day. At the stroke of midnight, the celebrations stop and Lent begins. The contrast of the carnival feasting and merriment with the austerity of the Lenten fasting period highlights the conflict between the demands of the material world and the spiritual life.

People dress up in colorful costumes and take part in street parades and parties during the Maastricht Carnival.

EASTER

The Easter and Whitsun holidays usually fall in March or April each year. Devout Christians attend a church service on Good Friday evening and another on Easter Sunday.

On Easter, children play games with easter eggs. Parents hide chocolate eggs and candies all over the house and garden, and children have a merry time hunting for them. In another Dutch game called *eiertikken* (eh-yer-TIK-ken), children bump their decorated eggs together to see whose will break first.

CHRISTMAS AND NEW YEAR

The Christmas season runs from the feast of St. Nicholas on December 5 to Christmas Day. Until quite recently, the celebrations focused solely on Saint Nicholas, or Sinterklaas (SIN-ter-klahs), as the Dutch call him.

Sinterklaas, dressed here like a bishop, parades through the crowded streets of Amsterdam.

According to tradition, Sinterklaas leaves Spain at the end of November, on a boat with his Moorish attendant, Zwarte Piet (ZWAR-teh peet, or Black Peter), who is usually represented by a white person with his or her face painted black. When Sinterklaas and Zwarte Piet arrive in Amsterdam, they are welcomed with great ceremony by the mayor. Then, seated on a white horse and dressed as a bishop, Sinterklaas leads a procession through the city.

Zwarte Piet distributes sweets to the children in the crowd who have been good. He also carries a cane to punish children who have been naughty, but of course he never uses it.

Interestingly, the American Santa Claus was born out of the Dutch Sinterklaas. Americans learned about Sinterklaas from Dutch immigrants who brought their Christmas traditions to the United States. Since the Dutch pronunciation of Sinterklaas was difficult to grasp, in time he became known as Santa Claus. An American poet, Clement C. Moore, created the figure of a jolly, fat man dressed in red in "A Visit from St. Nicholas", and Santa Claus then became known to the rest of the world.

On the eve of St. Nicholas's Day, December 5, families gather together. The children are usually very excited, knowing that Sinterklaas has arrived in the Netherlands and will be coming to their homes. They put their shoes on the fireplace at night for their presents and also add a little gift for Sinterklaas's horse, such as a carrot or some water. During the night, small gifts are put into the shoes, and the carrots and water disappear.

Adults also join in the fun by giving each other small, sometimes humorous presents, and writing amusing poems about each other. Traditionally the verses are supposed to be anonymous, but they are usually written by the donor of the present. It is now possible to buy ready-written poems or even hire a poet to write them. The poems are not always flattering—they tease people by referring to habits that others find annoying. But all this is lighthearted humor and taken in good spirits.

Christmas Day is a quiet occasion, with a family feast featuring meat, or fish, or game such as hare and venison. Traditionally, no gifts are exchanged during Christmas, although some families may do so following the American tradition.

New Year's Eve is an occasion for partying and celebrations. Church bells ring, fireworks displays take place, and in the harbors ships sound their sirens to welcome the New Year.

Speculaas (SPAY-koo-lahs) are spicy, dark brown biscuits made in molds during Christmas.

CULTURAL FESTIVALS AND FLORAL PARADES

The Netherlands enjoys a wide variety of festive events involving flowers, cheese, windmills, music and jazz, kite flying, and many other activities. Some are staged as one-time events, but many, like the Holland Festival, take place on an annual basis. A few have long histories, but most have been created since World War II.

The Holland Festival is held every year in June and July and is an officially sponsored event. It features plays, concerts, ballet, music, dance, and exhibitions, and draws leading international artists and groups, as well as lesser-known names from home and abroad. A deliberately contemporary program distinguishes it from other European festivals.

The first Holland Festival was held in 1947, and the event came to be rated as one of the best of its kind in Europe. But living up to that kind

Right: **A car decorated with flowers and vegetables takes part in a parade.**

Opposite: **Detail of a float decorated with fruits and vegetables.**

of success is a big problem, and some people feel that standards have dropped in recent years.

The North Sea Jazz Festival, held in The Hague every July, is growing more and more popular. It has been called the best jazz festival outside the United States. Utrecht has a Festival of Old Music covering music from the Middle Ages to the Romantic era.

Flower festivals continue to thrive and are always popular, as are the numerous flower parades. They are held all over the country but are mostly local affairs. August and September are the best flower-festival months, and cities and towns are filled with colorful floats, extravagantly decorated with thousands of blooms. One festival specializes in vegetables and harvest products and is especially attractive.

Processions of floats wend their way through the streets in a blaze of color, accompanied by bands, cheerleaders, and trick cyclists. Aalsmeer claims to have the largest festival. Its floats go on show on a Friday, the parade is held on a Saturday, and the floats can be viewed again on Sunday. The oldest flower pageant is held at Zundert near the border with Belgium. This pageant draws many flower lovers, who come to see the best display of dahlias in the country.

Other interesting regional festivals include the International Firework Festival held in August in The Hague, and craft festivals and horse fairs in the other provinces.

FOOD

Numerous pictures painted in the 17th century reveal that winters in the Netherlands were much harsher than they generally are today. Icy winds blew across the polders, the canals froze solid, and the Dutch ate large, hearty meals—high in fats and carbohydrates—to provide themselves with energy and keep themselves warm. Popular foods were thick pea soup, mashed vegetable dishes, and nourishing meat stews. To some extent, this tradition continues, although meals are simpler now, and portions are smaller than they were in the past.

Dutch food is plainly cooked and wholesome, with plenty of bread, vegetables, fruit, and dairy products. Protein is supplied primarily by meat and fish and, of course, lots of home-produced cheese. Dutch women do not slave over hot stoves any longer than is absolutely necessary. Their cooking is geared toward dishes that are easy to prepare.

VEGETABLES, MEAT, AND FISH

Winter or summer vegetables abound, and they are either grown in the fields or raised in the greenhouses that cover so much of South Holland. Dutch cooks can count on endless supplies of potatoes and curly kale, onions and carrots, spinach and peas, squash, several types of green and white beans, and a wide range of vegetables for salads. Less common items, such as asparagus, fennel, artichokes, and eggplant, are also available. There are also plentiful supplies of fish, including salmon and trout, and seafood, such as lobster, shrimp, and scallops.

Above: **A wide variety of seafood is available in the Netherlands.**

Opposite: **Each summer, cheese markets in Gouda sell all types of Dutch cheeses, attracting crowds that come not just for the dairy products but also for the festive atmosphere.**

Office workers usually have a light lunch consising of a sandwich and a beverage in a cafeteria.

EATING HABITS

Breakfast (called *ontbijt*, or ont-BAYD) is a bread-and-butter affair in the Netherlands. The table is laden with several different kinds of bread and a variety of toppings—thin slices of smoked beef or other cold meats, sausages, tinned fish, preserves, and cheese. These are used to make open sandwiches with slices of bread—from plain white loaves, golden whole wheat, and heavy black rye bread, to tasty raisin and seed bread. Sometimes there may be croissants, crunchy dried bread, currant rolls, and *ontbijkoek* (ont-BAYD-kook)—a spiced bread flavored with dark brown sugar, molasses, ground cloves, cinnamon, ginger, and nutmeg.

Lunch is similar, although there may be a warm dish—perhaps a vegetable soup, an omelet, or the popular *uitsmijter* (OUTS-may-ter). This is an open sandwich of buttered bread generously topped with thinly sliced roast beef or ham, and crowned by two fried eggs. The name *uitsmijter* literally means "chucker out." It came about many years back when it was dreamed up as a farewell snack for the end of a party. A tasty and filling quick snack, it is served in lunch bars and cafés all over the Netherlands.

Lunch was formerly the main meal of the day, but with changing lifestyles and with more people working regular office hours, the Dutch now have their main meal early in the evening, at around 6 or 7 P.M. However, farmers who start work at dawn and others who find it more convenient to eat the main meal earlier still do so around midday. Throughout the day, people have several breaks for tea or coffee with a cookie or, as a special treat, a piece of cake or some chocolate.

THE MAIN MEAL OF THE DAY

The main meal of the day, be it lunch or dinner, often begins with a substantial vegetable soup. Occasionally a thinner bouillon with meat-balls or noodles is served. Other appetizers might be fresh grapefruit or a small, cold dish.

A family having a dinner of soup and bread.

The main course includes fish or meat with vegetables. Potatoes are almost always served. The Dutch value the texture and flavor even of the plain, boiled potato and eat a lot of them with their main meal. They boil or steam potatoes with a small amount of water in a pan with a tightly fitting lid. When all the liquid has been absorbed, the potatoes are shaken in the pan until they are flaky and dry.

Mashed potatoes are prepared with milk, nutmeg, and butter or margarine, then beaten until they are white and creamy. Occasionally they are dotted with butter and browned under the grill or in the oven. Potato salad is made with freshly boiled potatoes dressed with a mustard, onion, vinegar, and mayonnaise sauce, and garnished with chopped parsley. For something special, small pears poached in spiced red wine are a popular side dish.

Desserts tend to be fairly simple. They include fruit, ice cream, fruit pies, and bread-based puddings made with eggs and dried fruit. Pancakes are also popular and, like pies and puddings, are often served with cream.

The Dutch say Eet smakelijk *(eight SMA-keh-luck) when starting a meal, literally meaning "Enjoy your meal!"*

123

DUTCH CHEESE

Unlike Great Britain, where cheese is often eaten for dessert, cheese is an important part of breakfast and lunch in the Netherlands but seldom appears at the main meal.

The Dutch have been making cheese since before the Middle Ages, and with modern methods, the Netherlands is now one of Europe's leading cheese makers.

Milk arriving in large tanker trucks at the cheese factory is held in vast stainless steel vats, where it is heated or pasteurized to kill harmful bacteria. The fat content of the milk is then reduced, sometimes by use of a centrifuge, depending on the type of cheese to be made. In the case of Gouda cheese, for example, the milk is skimmed to a fat content of 3.5 percent. The milk is then ready for making cheese, a process that is now controlled by computer.

The milk is transferred to a curd-making unit, in which the curd is separated from the fluid by coagulation. The whey (fluid) is sucked off, and the remaining curd is pressed into molds. Finally, it is immersed in a brine bath for several days, and then dried and packed. In a modern cheese factory, 5,000 cheeses, each weighing about 25 pounds (11 kg), can be made daily.

Some cheeses are round, others are loaf-shaped. The best-known varieties outside the Netherlands are Gouda (HOW-dah) and Edam (AY-dam). Gouda is round like a cartwheel with bulging sides, and Edam cheese has a cannonball shape with a waxy red coating. This originated from the custom of dipping the cheeses intended for sale in a protective wax covering. Nowadays, the protective coating is often supplemented by a red cellophane wrapper.

Of the 550 million tons (495 metric tons) of cheese produced each year in the Netherlands, 98 percent comes from over 50 highly automated factories.

SPECIALTIES

Popular Dutch dishes include minced meatballs, beans and bacon, and chicken served with applesauce. Smoked sausage is used in *erwtensoep* (ERT-en-soop)—a thick winter soup made from peas—or in hashes of mashed potatoes and other vegetables.

The Dutch have many tasty stews. The simplest is a combination of beef, potatoes, onions, and carrots. There is also the rich Hunter's Dish, with layers of stewed venison, sliced potato, apples, and fried onions. Sometimes it is made into a kind of pie by omitting the potato slices and replacing them with a topping of mashed potato.

Another Dutch specialty is the pancake. These are usually the size of dinner plates—about 12 inches (30 cm) in diameter—and are made with yeast. They come in two varieties—dinner pancakes served with smoked sausage or bacon, and sweet ones topped with a rich syrup, apples and cream, or ice cream. A favorite dessert is a custard called *vla* (vlah) that comes in several fruit flavors, chocolate, and vanilla. For other desserts, there are waffles and *poffertjes* (POF-er-tches). *Poffertjes* are small, round doughnuts without a hole or a filling, sprinkled with confectioner's sugar.

Eating *poffertjes* at a roadside stall.

DRINKS

When having a drink with Dutch people, it is customary to raise one's glass and wish them *Proost* (prost) or *Gezondheid* (heh-ZONT-hayt), meaning "Your health. This is the equivalent of saying "Cheers!"

The national drink is a gin called *jenever* (jeh-NAY-ver), which comes in two varieties—*jonge* (yong, or young) which is almost colorless, and *oude* (owd, or old), which is pale yellow and stronger. Both are drunk undiluted and in small quantities. People who prefer a lighter drink have beer, wine, or fruit liqueurs such as apricot or cherry brandy.

When it comes to beer, which almost everyone drinks, the most popular variety is a light brew. Some Dutch beers, such as Heineken, are sold all over the world. Wine is sometimes drunk with meals. Common after-dinner drinks include a creamy eggnog called Advocaat or a bourbon.

Friends enjoying a drink at a roadside café.

SEASONAL FOODS

April is the time for plovers' eggs, young asparagus begins to appear in May, and the oyster and mussel season begins in July. Autumn and winter bring a demand for game, especially wild boar.

At the start of the herring season each spring, fishing boats compete to bring back the first boatload of herring. By tradition, the first barrel of new herring is always presented to the queen.

ERWTENSOEP (DUTCH PEA SOUP)

This thick, rich soup is extremely filling and is a very popular dish in winter. When the soup is cold, it becomes almost solid, but it reheats well.

2 cups green split peas
3 quarts (3 liters) cold water
1/2 cup thickly cut bacon, roughly chopped
2 leeks, cut into short lengths
1 diced celeriac, or 2 stalks celery, diced
2 tablespoons chopped celery leaves
1 pound (1/2 kg) potatoes, peeled and sliced
2 chopped onions
Salt
4 hot dogs, cut into chunks

Wash the peas and soak for 12 hours, unless using quick-cooking peas. Then simmer for at least two hours. Add the bacon and simmer for another hour. Add the vegetables and salt to taste. Continue simmering until all the vegetables are cooked and the soup is smooth and thick (about 45 minutes). Add the hot dogs in the last 10 minutes. Adjust seasonings and serve.

REGIONAL FOODS

Different provinces also have special dishes. In the southern Catholic areas, fish is widely served and is often eaten on Fridays. A great deal of fish and seafood is also consumed in the coastal provinces. Further inland, and especially in the northern polders where cattle, pigs, and chickens are bred, meat is eaten in larger quantities.

Specific dishes are often associated with individual towns. The people of Arnhem, for instance, have a casserole similar to Hungarian goulash, while *vla*, also known as Limburg pies—a thin, flat pie filled with fruit—is named after the southernmost province. Another delightful dessert is The Hague Bluff. As residents of The Hague are often thought by other Dutch people to be showing off, the light and fluffy Hague Bluff—made from no more than fruit syrup, sugar, and an egg white—is associated with their elegant city.

Brown cafés have been described as a cross between a British pub and a French café. They serve inexpensive food and drink.

EATING OUT AND FAST FOOD

Sometimes work and other conditions leave little time to prepare and eat food at home. This presents few problems for the Dutch, who can take their pick of cheap and tasty snacks from street stalls and cafés. If they feel like treating themselves to something exotic, then the Indonesian *rijsttafel* (RAYS-tah-fel, meaning rice table), fits the bill.

The ever-popular *uitsmijter* probably comes at the top of the list of quick snacks, but it is closely followed by numerous varieties of filled *broodjes* (BROH-tches), or soft bread rolls. These are the Netherlands' equivalent of an American sandwich. Sandwich fillings are almost the same as those for breakfast and lunch, but sometimes with more expensive items like steak tartare, shrimp, and spiced ground beef. In the bigger towns, plain rolls are sometimes replaced by stuffed croissants.

Other fast-food snacks include French fries with mayonnaise, and pancakes garnished with bacon or ham.

A TASTE OF THE EAST

The Dutch tell a joke about one of their compatriots who complained that a restaurant had only fancy foreign food on the menu. He especially complained about the lack of good old Dutch fare like his favorite *rijsttafel*. This story illustrates the extent to which Indonesian food (such as this man's beloved *rijsttafel*) has been absorbed into the Netherlands.

The *rijsttafel* comprises a selection of spicy dishes served with steamed rice and accompanied by fiery *sambals* (SAHM-bahls) which is a strong chilli paste, and side dishes of hard-boiled eggs, shrimp, and other items. Many dishes are cooked in coconut milk, spiced with ground coriander, cumin, and yellow turmeric, and flavored with sesame oil or soy sauce. Other ingredients include pungent dried-shrimp paste and lemongrass.

An Indonesian *satay* seller. Immigrants from former Dutch colonies have introduced exotic, spicy dishes to the Netherlands.

A simple meal might have as few as half a dozen dishes, while a banquet could have 16 and 30 dishes with a selection of meat and vegetable curries.

Beef *rendang* (REHN-dahng) is a favorite on most menus, together with *panggang* (PAHNG-gahng, or barbecued) pork, chicken, and fish served with mild to red-hot sauces. Vegetables can be cooked in coconut milk with curry spices or served as *gado gado* (gah-doh gah-doh), a salad with a peanut sauce. A similar peanut sauce accompanies *satay* (SAH-teh), grilled meat on skewers garnished with slices of cucumber and raw onion.

DRAADJESVLEES (BEEF STEW)

2 pounds beef chuck, cut into large chunks
salt
pepper
2 tablespoons butter
3 cups hot water
$\frac{1}{3}$ cup red wine
4 cloves
1 bay leaf
1 tomato, chopped
1 onion, peeled and chopped

Rub beef with salt and pepper. Over medium heat, melt butter and sauté beef until browned. Add water, wine, cloves, bay leaf, tomato, and onion. Simmer for two hours or until the beef is soft and falling apart. Serve with boiled potatoes and vegetables.

BITTERKOEKJES PUDDING (ALMOND COOKIE PUDDING)

A bowl of cold water
1 pack *bitterkoekjes* (or almond cookies)
$^1/_2$ quart ($^1/_2$ liter) milk
4 egg yolks
2 $^1/_2$ tablespoons of granulated gelatin
2 egg whites
$^1/_2$ cups sugar
1 cup heavy cream
$^1/_4$ cup raspberry jam

Crumble the cookies after drying them out on a low-heat in an oven, at about 250°F (120°C). Bring the milk just to a boil, then soak the crumbled cookies in the milk. In a separate bowl, mix the egg yolks with the sugar. With a whisk, beat this mixture until it forms a thick, pale cream. Add this creamy mixture to the milk and cookies. Heat this over a pan of water that is brought just to a boil. Whisk the mixture to make it creamier. Stir the gelatin into the mixture. This will start to set. Take the egg whites and whisk until very stiff. Also whisk the double cream until it

becomes moderately thick. Fold in the whisked double cream and egg whites into the pudding. Place the final mixture into a mold and let it set for 6 hours in the fridge or in a cool place. Serve by drizzling heated raspberry jam.

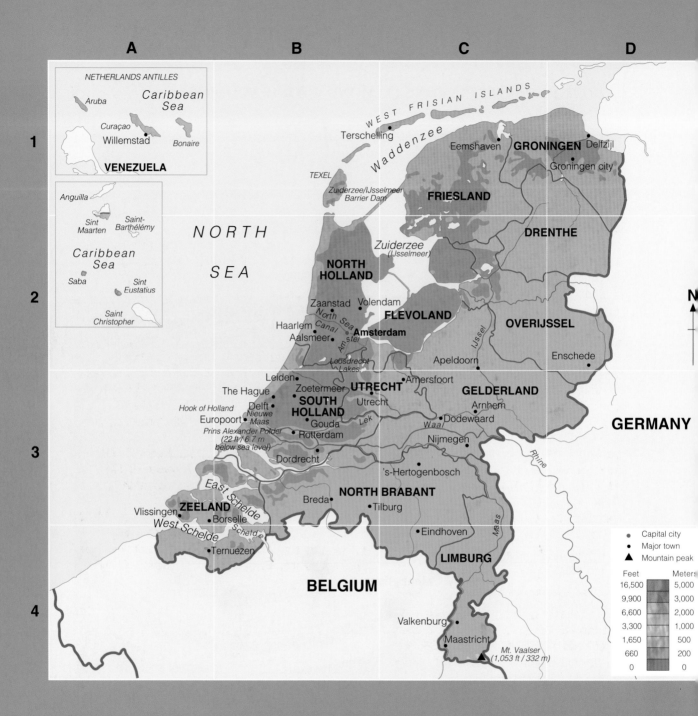

A **B** **C** **D**

NETHERLANDS ANTILLES

Caribbean Sea

Aruba

Curaçao Willemstad *Bonaire*

1

VENEZUELA

Anguilla

Sint Maarten *Saint-Barthélémy*

Caribbean Sea

Saba *Sint Eustatius*

Saint Christopher

NORTH

SEA

2

3

4

WEST FRISIAN ISLANDS

Terschelling
Waddenzee
Eemshaven **GRONINGEN** Delfzijl

TEXEL
Groningen city

Zuiderzee/IJsselmeer Barrier Dam
FRIESLAND

DRENTHE

Zuiderzee (IJsselmeer)

NORTH HOLLAND

Zaanstad Volendam

Haarlem *North Canal* **FLEVOLAND**
Aalsmeer **Amsterdam** *Amstel*

OVERIJSSEL

IJssel

Enschede

Apeldoorn

Leiden *Loosdrecht Lakes*

The Hague Zoetermeer **UTRECHT** Amersfoort **GELDERLAND**

Delft **SOUTH HOLLAND** Utrecht

Hook of Holland *Nieuwe Maas* *Lek* Arnhem

Europoort Gouda Dodewaard

Prins Alexander Polder (22 ft / 6.7 m below sea level) Rotterdam *Waal*

Nijmegen

Dordrecht

Rhine

's-Hertogenbosch

East Schelde Breda **NORTH BRABANT**

Vlissingen **ZEELAND** Tilburg

Borselle *Schelde*

West Schelde Eindhoven

Ternuezen *Maas*

LIMBURG

BELGIUM

Valkenburg

Maastricht

Mt. Vaalser (1,053 ft / 332 m)

GERMANY

N

● Capital city
● Major town
▲ Mountain peak

Feet	Meters
16,500	5,000
9,900	3,000
6,600	2,000
3,300	1,000
1,650	500
660	200
0	0

MAP OF THE NETHERLANDS

ECONOMIC NETHERLANDS

Agriculture

- Dairy Products
- Flowers

Manufacturing

- Industrial Complex
- Diamond Cutting

Services

- Port

ABOUT
THE ECONOMY

OVERVIEW

The Netherlands is a highly industrialized nation. Trade based on the transit of goods accounts for more than half the country's income. The Netherlands is the third largest exporter of agricultural goods in the world, and the largest exporter of dairy products.

GROSS DOMESTIC PRODUCT (GDP)

US$481.1 billion (2004)

GDP BY SECTOR

Agriculture 2.4 percent, industry 24.5 percent, services 73.1 percent (2004)

AREA

Total: 16,033 square miles (41,526 square km)
Land: 13,082 square miles (33,883 square km)
Water: 2,951 square miles (7,643 square km)

LAND USE

Arable 27 percent, permanent crops 1 percent, forest 11 percent

CURRENCY

1 euro (EUR) = 100 cents
USD 1 = EUR 0.8
Notes: 5, 10, 20, 50, 100, 200, 500
Coins: 1, 2, 5, 10, 20, and 50 cents; 1 and 2 euros

AGRICULTURAL PRODUCTS

Sugar beets, fruit, vegetables, flowers, potatoes, grains, livestock

NATURAL RESOURCES

Petroleum, natural gas, arable land

POPULATION

16.3 million (2005 estimate)

WORKFORCE

7.53 million (2004)

WORKFORCE BY SECTOR

Agriculture 4 percent, industry 23 percent, services 73 percent

UNEMPLOYMENT RATE

6 percent (2004)

PORTS AND HARBORS

Amsterdam, Delfzijl, Dordrecht, Eemshaven, Groningen, Haarlem, IJmuiden, Maastricht, Rotterdam, Terneuzen, Utrecht, Vlissingen

MAJOR EXPORTS

Machinery, transportation equipment, food, chemicals, flowers, electrical equipment

MAJOR TRADE PARTNERS

Germany, Belgium, United Kingdom, France, United States, Italy, China

MAJOR IMPORTS

Clothing, foods, chemicals, fuels, machinery, transportation equipment

CULTURAL NETHERLANDS

Volendam
Traditional dress is still worn here on a daily basis.

Friesland
People here speak Frisian, which is more similar to Old English than to Dutch.

Amsterdam
The Rijkmuseum, the most important museum in the Netherlands, houses art by Flemish, Dutch, Italian, and Spanish masters from the 15th to the 19th centuries.

Leiden
The oldest university in the Netherlands was founded here in 1575.

Delft
Delft is famous for its blue and white pottery called Delftware.

The Hague
This is the seat of the government. The North Sea Jazz Festival is held here every July.

Valkenburg
Valkenburg Castle, the only castle built on an elevation in the Netherlands, dates back to the Middle Ages.

ABOUT THE CULTURE

COUNTRY NAME
Kingdom of the Netherlands

CAPITAL
Amsterdam

FLAG DESCRIPTION
Three equal horizontal bands of red, white, and blue. One of the oldest flags in continuous use, it originated with William I, Prince of Orange, in the 16th century. The flag sometimes has an orange piece of fabric (*de wimpel*) on top as a reminder of the House of Orange.

LANGUAGES
Dutch. There are also several dialects, named after the regions in which they are spoken. Frisian is a separate language, spoken in the province of Friesland and not understood by ordinary Dutch-speakers.

ETHNIC GROUPS
Dutch descent 83 percent, non-Western descent 9 percent, other 8 percent

LIFE EXPECTANCY
Men 76 years, women 82 years

LITERACY RATE
99 percent

RELIGIONS
Christianity 91 percent; Islam 6 percent; Hinduism, Judaism, and Buddhism 3 percent

EDUCATION
Full-time school is compulsory from ages 5 to 16 and paid for by the government. Most schools are coeducational.

LEADERS IN POLITICS
Prince William of Orange, Queen Beatrix, Jan Peter Balkenende (prime minister of the Netherlands since 2002)

IMPORTANT LITERARY FIGURES
Erasmus (translated the New Testament from Greek to Latin), Gerbrand Adriaensz Bredero (poet and playwright during the Dutch Golden Age), Joost van den Vondel (dramatist and national poet in the 17th century), Harry Mulisch (20th-century writer), Anne Frank (Dutch Jewish diarist, victim of Nazi persecution)

IMPORTANT SCHOLARS
Thomas-a-Kempis (religious author), Hugo Grotius (author in international law, theologian, statesman, and poet), Baruch Spinoza (philosopher)

IMPORTANT ARTISTS
Rembrandt van Rijn, Vincent van Gogh, Jan Vermeer, Jan Steen, Frans Hals, Piet Mondriaan

TIME LINE

IN THE NETHERLANDS	IN THE WORLD
	753 B.C. Rome is founded.
	116–17 B.C. The Roman empire reaches its greatest extent, under Emperor Trajan (98–17).
First century B.C. Maastricht is a Roman settlement.	
A.D. 100 The Frisians, a Teutonic tribe, settle in what is now the Netherlands.	
	A.D. 600 Height of Mayan civilization
A.D. 800 Frisians accept Christianity from the Franks, a conglomeration of German tribes.	**1000** The Chinese perfect gunpowder and begin to use it in warfare.
1489–90 The Netherlands is ravaged by the plague.	**1530** Beginning of trans-Atlantic slave trade organized by the Portuguese in Africa.
	1558–1603 Reign of Elizabeth I of England
1620 Dutch pilgrims board the *Mayflower* to complete their journey to America.	
1626 Dutch explorer Peter Minuit takes over the island of Manhattan and the southern part of the island is named Nieuw Amsterdam.	
1600–1700s The Dutch colonize what is now Indonesia, naming it the Dutch East Indies.	**1776** U.S. Declaration of Independence
	1789–99 The French Revolution
	1861 The U.S. Civil War begins.
	1869 The Suez Canal is opened.
1914–18 The Dutch remain neutral during World War I.	**1914** World War I begins.
1939 The Dutch declare their neutrality.	**1939** World War II begins.

IN THE NETHERLANDS	IN THE WORLD
1940–45	
The Germans air-bomb Rotterdam, and the Netherlands surrenders. The royal family flees to England. Nazi occupation ends with Germany's surrender to the Allies in 1945.	
1945	**1945**
The Netherlands is a charter member of the United Nations.	The United States drops atomic bombs on Hiroshima and Nagasaki.
1949	**1949**
The Dutch East Indies, which Japan occupied during the war, gains independence as Indonesia.	The North Atlantic Treaty Organization (NATO) is formed.
1952	
The Netherlands is a founding member of the European Coal and Steel Community, which evolves into the present European Union.	**1957**
	The Russians launch Sputnik.
1975	**1966–69**
Surinam achieves independence from the Dutch.	The Chinese Cultural Revolution
1980	
Queen Beatrix succeeds Queen Juliana as queen of the Netherlands.	**1986**
	Nuclear power disaster at Chernobyl in Ukraine
	1991
	Break-up of the Soviet Union
	1997
	Hong Kong is returned to China.
2000	
The Netherlands legalizes euthanasia.	
2001	**2001**
Same-sex couples are allowed to get married and adopt children.	Terrorists crash planes in New York, Washington, D.C., and Pennsylvania.
2002	
The guilder is replaced by the euro. Jan Peter Balkenende becomes the prime minister.	
2003	**2003**
The Netherlands sends more than 1,500 troops to Iraq to support the U.S. troops there.	War in Iraq

GLOSSARY

Algemeen Beschaafd Nederlands (AHL-heh-main Behs-SHAAHFT NAY-der-lands)
The standard Dutch language that is used for official purposes and is taught in schools.

dike
A levee or river bank built of earth, used to control flooding of rivers or the sea.

Europoort (YEW-ROH-port)
A complex of docks, berths, warehouses, and basins that line the mouth of the Niewe Maas river from Rotterdam to the North Sea. It is the world's largest port complex.

formateur (form-a-TERH)
The ruling party leader who forms the government; the *formateur* usually becomes prime minister.

gezelligheid (gheh-ZEL-ligh-hayd)
A cozy, warm atmosphere in Dutch homes.

gracht (grahcht)
Canal

hofjes (HOFF-yehs)
Homes for senior citizens.

klompen (KLOM-pen)
Dutch clogs, still commonly worn when doing heavy or dirty work.

Mijnheer (mehn-NEER)
Mister

Mevrouw (mehv-FRAOW)
Mistress (Mrs.)

ontbijt (ont-BAYD)
Breakfast, which is usually a meal of bread and butter.

polder (POHL-der)
An area of low-lying land that has been reclaimed from the sea or other body of water.

Randstadt (ROHN-stadt)
The densely populated area of North and South Holland; incorporates Amsterdam, Rotterdam, Haarlem, Utrecht, Leiden, and The Hague.

rijsttafel (RAYS-tah-fel)
An Indonesian buffet-type meal where rice is served with many other dishes of meat, fish, and vegetables.

States General
The Dutch parliament, comprising the Upper and Lower House.

verzuilen (ver-ZUEH-len)
The pillarization system, where people and society are distinguished by the different systems of beliefs, or pillars, to which they belong.

voetbal (VOOT-bahl)
Soccer, the most popular sport in the Netherlands

FURTHER INFORMATION

BOOKS

Grattan, Thomas Colley. *Holland: The History of the Netherlands*. Whitefish, MT: Kessinger Publishing, 2004.

Janin, Hunt. *Culture Shock! Netherlands*. Portland, OR: Graphic Arts Center Publishing Co., 2003.

Steves, Rick and Steve Smith. *Rick Steves' France, Belgium and the Netherlands 2002*. Emeryville, CA: Avalon Travel Publishing, 2002.

White, Colin and Laurie Boucke. *The UnDutchables: An Observation of the Netherlands, Its Culture and Its Inhabitants*. Lafayette, IN: White-Boucke Publishing, 2001.

WEB SITES

Central Intelligience Agency World Factbook (select the Netherlands from country list).
www.cia.gov/cia/publications/factbook.html

Country Reports. www.countryreports.org

Healthcare in the Netherlands. www.minbuza.nl. Select English language option.

Immigration and Integration in the Netherlands. www.fpc.org.uk/articles/149

Largest Urban Areas of the European Union.
www.answers.com/topic/largest-urban-areas-of-the-european-union

Lonely Planet: Explore the World. www.lonelyplanet.com/destinations

The Netherlands: International Religious Freedom Report 2004. U.S. Department of State.
www.state.gov/g/drl/rls/irf/2004/35475.htm

The Royal Netherlands Embassy, Washington, DC. www.netherlands-embassy.org

Social and Cultural Planning Office of the Netherlands www.scp.nl/english

Sports in the Netherlands. www.answers.com/topic/sport-in-the-netherlands

BIBLIOGRAPHY

Bijlsma, Rob G. and Frank E. de Roder. "Nest-building ospreys Pandion Haliaetus in the Ostvaardersplassen in the late Summer. 2002." *De Takkeling*, Nov. 2002.

Catling, Christopher. *Insight Guides Holland*. New York: Insight Guides, 2003.

Ewart, Jane. *Holland* (Eyewitness Travel Guides). London: Dorling Kindersley, 2003.

Frank, Anne. *Anne Frank: The Diary of a Young Girl*, New York: Modern Library Inc., 1994.

Ian, James. *The Netherlands*. New York: F. Watts, 1990.

Lerner Publications Co. *Netherlands—in Pictures*. Minneapolis, MN: Lerner Publications Co., 1991.

Lucas, Eileen. *Vincent van Gogh*. New York: F. Watts, 1991.

Martin, Dunford. *The Rough Guide to the Netherlands*. New York: Rough Guides, 2003.

Schwartz, Gary. *Rembrandt*. New York: H.N. Abrams, 1992.

Stegeren, Theo van. *The Land and People of the Netherlands*. New York: Harper Collins, 1991.

INDEX

143